Bertolt Brecht: Diaries 1920–1922

Edited by HERTA RAMTHUN

Translated and annotated by JOHN WILLETT

Brecht's Plays, Poetry and Prose
annotated and edited in hardback by
John Willett and Ralph Manheim

Brecht in paperback in Methuen's
Modern Plays *(paperback editions of
the annotated Collected Plays are
superseding the existing unannotated
editions)*

Bertolt Brecht Diaries

1920–1922

Edited by
Herta Ramthun

Translated and annotated with an
introductory essay by John Willett

ST. MARTIN'S PRESS
NEW YORK

Library of Congress Cataloging in Publication Data

Brecht, Bertolt, 1898-1956.
  Diaries 1920-1922.

  Translation of Tagebücher 1920-1922.
  1. Brecht, Bertolt, 1898-1956—Diaries. 2. Authors,
German—20th century—Biography. I. Ramthun, Herta.
II. Willett, John. III. Title.
PT2603.R397Z52513   1979   838′.9′1203   78-21345
ISBN 0-312-07703-3

Contents

List of illustrations

All photos are reproduced by courtesy of Werner Frisch, Augsburg, except no. 8c, which is by courtesy of the Brecht-Archiv, East Berlin.

Introduction

When Brecht started keeping his diary in June 1920 he was unknown outside a small circle of Augsburg and Munich friends. His only published writings had appeared in the local Augsburg papers, where he contributed the occasional poem but figured more often as a harsh and self-assured critic of productions at the municipal theatre. And yet he already had a strong sense of his own significance. 'Though I am only 22', says a note made just before the diaries proper begin,

> and have grown up in the small city of Augsburg on the Lech without having seen more than a fraction of the earth – apart from the meadows, that is, just this city with its trees and one or two other cities, though never for long – I am seized with a wish to have the whole world delivered to me: I wish all things to be handed over to *me*, along with power over all animals; and my grounds for this demand are that I shall exist only *once*.

Much of the Brecht encountered in these entries is quite unlike the ruthless cynic of *The Threepenny Opera* or the didactic Marxist of the crisis years when Hitler came to power, let alone the reflective philosopher of East Berlin. He is ebullient, enjoying words for their own sake, caring little for other people's feelings or interests and less still for social or humanitarian causes; and his diary, unlike his 'Working Journal' (*Arbeitsjournal*) from 1938 on, is written without thought of possible publication. The sardonic, paradoxical twist is already unmistakeable: 'Life as a passion! That's how I conduct it', he exclaims in another note, adding 'Clearly it's one that will be the death of me'. But never again was he so openly interested in himself.

The Brecht whom we meet here is at a crucial stage in his life, some two years before his first great success with *Drums in the Night*. For most of the time he is living as a medical student in Munich, but spending his weekends and holidays at home in

Augsburg some fifty miles away. 'Home' is the attic floor of the house in the Bleichstrasse where his father lives, looked after by Marie Roecker the family housekeeper. His younger brother Walter is usually away, studying to follow their father into the management of the Haindl paper mills (to whom the house belongs), but most of their Augsburg friends of both sexes are still around in one or other of the two ancient cities. Brecht goes for walks by the river Lech or the old town moat, strolls under the chestnut trees scribbling on folded sheets of paper, visits the Plärrer, the local fairground, or sprawls in the lush meadows; once he spends a week with his friends walking through the Swabian countryside from which his family of teachers, doctors and printers originally came. In a great burst of creativity starting in 1918 he has already written many of his finest early poems as well as the first two versions of *Baal*, a kind of dramatic resumé of all this poetry, set against the beauties of the south German landscape. *Baal* has been submitted to the Munich Residenz-Theater, a wonderful eighteenth-century house which the Bavarian Revolution of 1919 placed under the direction of the actor Albert Steinrück, and has also been accepted for publication by the Munich firm of Georg Müller. A second, more deliberately commercial play called *Drums in the Night* is with his literary mentor Lion Feuchtwanger, who is about to send it to the Kammerspiele, smallest of the Munich state theatres. At home Brecht is still known as Eugen, the problem son of a respected business man and amateur choral singer. In his criticisms for the local Independent Socialist (USPD) paper he is already the opinionated but undoubtedly gifted BB.

Nor is there much doubt which way he will go. The main motive for his medical studies had fairly clearly been the need to keep him out of the army as long as possible, and it vanished with the ending of the war in November 1918, only a month after he began his service as an orderly in a local hospital. Where once he was attending ten different classes or courses at the university he is now inscribed for only two, the one on anatomy and physiology, the other on the history of German literature. He is on the point of dropping out. But what is not yet certain is the form his career as a writer will take, and this only begins to become clear in the ensuing twenty months. The background of his poems (which was also that of *Baal*) then shifts from the rich countryside and the 'little boarded rooms' of village pubs to the gaunt severity of postwar Berlin; the first characteristic irregular unrhymed poems emerge in the shape of the Epistles of winter 1921–22, three of which are included in diary entries. His more or less Expressionist period, strongly influenced by Rimbaud and Wedekind, ends with the first version of *In the Jungle*, his third play, which he finished during 1922; the *Galgei* project on which he is working is put off, to be completed in quite different form after his final move to Berlin in 1924. Also in 1922 his first collection of poems is put together, though its actual appearance is delayed for some years as a result of his success with *Drums in the Night*, which would win him a major literary prize that autumn, thereby establishing him first and foremost as a playwright. At the time when we meet him however it seems quite possible that he will be known primarily as a poet, while he may even go over entirely to the still new medium of the film. For there are studios in Munich, where serials are being made featuring a detective called Stuart Webbs, and we can watch Brecht's efforts to break into this fascinating and lucrative field. When he fails the way is clear for him to concentrate mainly on the stage.

*

If this period was a turning-point for the young Brecht, so it was also for Bavaria and indeed for Germany as a whole. Before the recent war Munich, with its roughly half a million inhabitants (five times as many as Augsburg), had been one of the great European cultural centres: less important than Paris perhaps but rivalling Vienna and a good deal more brilliant and entertaining than Germany's still 'Prussian' imperial capital, Berlin. After 1918 Munich retained its state theatres, its great art collections and its important publishing houses, but it was no longer quite the city of Ibsen and Thomas Mann, of Frank Wedekind and the *Blaue Reiter*, of Jugendstil and Richard Strauss; and from then on its rôle in the arts declined. Whether this would have happened in any case is open to debate, but the decisive juncture seems to have been in the spring of 1919 when the Bavarian USPD premier Kurt Eisner was assassinated and his supporters' attempt to form a Soviet Republic brutally put down. For not only were a number of leading Munich intellectuals (including the anarchist writer Gustav Landauer and the poets Erich Mühsam and Ernst Toller) driven out, gaoled or even killed by the freebooting forces of law and order, but these very forces served to strengthen Hitler's newly formed Nazi party, which henceforward regarded Munich as the 'principal city of the movement'. With Prussia now transformed into the main stronghold of German Social-Democracy (and thereby of enlightened state patronage of the arts) Berlin was already much the more attractive town of the two, and henceforward the country's most influential theatres, publishers and critics were all to be found there. Thus in making his first, superficially rather unsuccessful attempt to conquer Berlin in the winter of 1921–22 Brecht was only following the trend of the times. But he also had a personal reason for distrusting the political reaction in Bavaria when the new administration finally turned down *Baal*.

Four months before the defeat of the Munich Soviet an ill-prepared Spartacist (i.e. Communist) rising had been crushed in Berlin with comparably fierce reprisals, notably the murder of its leaders Karl Liebknecht and Rosa Luxemburg. Though this had nothing like the same reactionary effects within the Prussian administration, the two events together made it clear that the German Revolution had reached its limits, stopping well short of any overthrow of the capitalist system. For much of the intellectual Left this was a great disillusionment, and it led to the widespread abandonment of the old Utopian Expressionism and to the adoption of a more hard-headedly pragmatic and cynical attitude towards both politics and art, soon to be summarised in the phrase 'new matter-of-factness' or *Neue Sachlichkeit*. Of course the country was far from settled, and there were still minor uprisings in different areas. Moreover the Allied occupation of the whole area west of the Rhine, along with the obligation to pay heavy reparations under the Versailles Treaty, gave industrialists and workers alike a paralysing sense of instability which had yet to come to its climax. It was only with its resolution after the great inflation of 1923 that the real flowering of the Weimar Republic and its culture could begin. But already there were symptoms of the impending change of climate, and it was Brecht's luck that these coincided with his first arrival on the Berlin scene. For a number of good judges there were dissatisfied with the Expressionist theatre, and what they saw of his unpublished writings suggested that he might well be what the new climate required.

*

The very first entries in the diary sketch the outlines. Here is the most creatively stimulating of all Brecht's friends, the designer Caspar Neher, whose contribution to his theatre was fundamental. But here too are a succession of terrible preoccupations: the rejection of *Baal*, the situation of his young mistress Bi Banholzer whose illegitimate child was then with foster-parents in the countryside, the need for a better ending for *Drums in the Night*, even the dental troubles familiar from some of his poems: all overshadowed by the recent death of his mother from a long and painful cancer. How much she had meant to him he never makes plain, though outside accounts suggest that it was she above all who had encouraged his literary and artistic interests. The poems and notes which he had been writing about her, however, already show his characteristic mixture of detachment, economy and insight. For instance there is a jotting which could have been for one of the 'Psalms' which he had recently taken to writing:

My mother died on the first of May. Spring arose. Shamelessly the heavens grinned.

– or such laconic observations as

Those were bones which they laid in a sheet. He left before earth had covered her over. Why watch what is self-evident?

– and the bitter-realistic epitaph 'I loved her in my way. But she wanted to be loved in hers'. Like so much else in Brecht's life and writings such comments seem to explain why he was so taken with the phrase which Julius Meier-Graefe had used about the painter Delacroix: 'a hot heart beating in a cold person'. Along with those other favourite sayings of his – 'Truth is concrete' and 'The proof of the pudding is in the eating' – it sums up much that was remarkable about him.

Far more than the (still untranslated) 'working journal' of some two decades later, the present diaries are personal ones, and much of their interest lies in finding out what kind of person the young Brecht was. There are surprises in store here for those who have some idea of the values and principles which he subsequently came to stand for, and even more for those who currently see him as providing answers to virtually any social or artistic problem of the present day. Thus he reveals himself (12 September 1920) to be sceptical about the Soviet dictatorship, and for remarkably far-sighted reasons; but he also dissociates himself from the plebeian crowd in a way that would have seemed contemptible to him later: 'the people, dumb, sinful and patient' who stand gaping at his beloved fairground. About Jews he speaks like any other young middle-class German or Austrian of his time; the fostering of utterly blind and cruel racial prejudice by the Nazis has not yet led such individuals to think more carefully and check their utterances, though these show how fertile the ground already was for racialist ideas. Similarly with the blacks, though here his allusions have to be seen in context: French African units were part of the occupying army in the Rhineland (where one of their bridgeheads took in Wiesbaden), while the rôle of the blacks in the entertainment industry was still such that the term 'negro' (music, acting etc.) could be pejoratively used. As for Brecht's attitude to women, this is even less likely to please his modern readers, since it is not merely unromantic in the extreme but based on a dreadful combination of possessiveness and sense of superiority. Time and again it manifests itself in more or less hair-raising comments, as when Bi Banholzer is discovered to have been going out with a musician, or when an unnamed girl keeps him waiting and is found guilty of being 'impolite'.

What makes his cliff-hanging love affair with Marianne Zoff so appallingly fascinating is its alternation of attitudes like this with evidence of a totally obsessive physical bond. On one plane she is not at all an appealing woman; she is not merely a provincial opera singer (i.e. everything that the later Brecht would have found most absurd) but is depicted, sometimes in cruel terms, as an unfastidious lover, accepting money gifts and betraying one man's intimacies to another. On the other – that of her Gauguinesque appearance and her physical harmony with Brecht – she is the living illustration of what he meant in *The Threepenny Opera* by 'sexual obsession', the *sexuelle Hörigkeit* which can tie a man to a woman against all his better judgement. He was a cool and detached enough observer to realise that this was an impossibly contradictory situation, and anyhow 'I can't get married. I must have elbowroom, be able to spit as I want, be unscrupulous'. Yet he hopes somehow to have things both ways, 'to be alone in bed and to have a woman in bed'; then only three weeks later he is proposing marriage to Bi Banholzer instead, complaining at the same time that 'nowadays she was always wanting her freedom'. The other great factor – perhaps the greatest – in impelling him towards marriage was his wish to be a father. True, he already had his son Frank whom neither Bi nor Marianne, nor for that matter Brecht's own father, seemed prepared to accept with anything like the affection which he felt in himself. But the decisive reason for his not marrying Marianne was her reluctance to bear his child, and when this changed a few months after the conclusion of these diaries they married after all. There is no reason to suppose that anything else in the relationship had changed, or that his harsh judgements of her no longer held good; and not surprisingly the marriage was short-lived. What seems much odder is the ending of his long affair with Bi, 'my youthful sweetheart' – so he termed her in a note of about 1930 – 'whom I was greatly attached to and who slipped away from me thanks to a strange indifference on my part'. By then she had married another man and had disappeared into the recesses of Brecht's memory 'like a figure in a book I had read'.

*

If the strangely mixed personality of Brecht himself is the unconscious theme of these pages, with his on-off relationship with Marianne furnishing the element of suspense, there is nevertheless a great deal here that sheds new light on his work. Apart from *Baal*, which he scarcely needed to touch, and *Edward II*, which he had not yet thought of tackling, this embraces all the early plays up to *Man equals Man*. *Drums in the Night* has been written, but his dissatisfaction with it is evident from the outset – 'a bad play' – and his nagging efforts to get the last act right continue throughout that summer; he wrote it, he later said, to make money, and this is borne out by his expectation (18 April 1921) of its earnings, for he counted on it to be more rewarding even than his film stories. *In the Jungle of Cities*, his third play, can be followed right from its genesis as a vague idea for 'a play of conflict' which occurred to him in mid-September of 1921, a month before he left Augsburg to join Marianne in occupied Wiesbaden and go on from there to Berlin. Here we can see its evident relation to the 'Ballad of the Love-Death' which he had just completed, and also to his feeling that nobody has yet written a *Jungle Book* of urban civilisation. This preoccupation with the savage and primitive nature of the big cities comes more and more to dominate him in the light of his experience of Berlin, whose immediate poetic impact can be traced in the 'Epistles'. Of course the Chicago depicted in the play bears scarcely any relation to the real city of that name; indeed when he used the term 'cold Chicago' that winter it was as a way of referring to Berlin. But he saw *In the Jungle* (as it was then called) as a way of establishing an urban mythology, contrasting it illuminatingly with *Baal*, the 'song of the countryside, its swansong'. From now on the conception of a trilogy called *Asphalt Jungle* or (as it later became) *Mankind's Occupation of the Great Cities* was to bulk large in his plans for many years. As for the 'song of the countryside' it was not heard again in his work until the writing of *Puntila* in Finland during the Second World War.

Running right through the period of the diary is the unfinished play called *Galgei*, a semi-farcical, very Bavarian drama about the malleability of human personality, with an extraordinary passive, massive, jellyfish-like 'lump of flesh' as its central character. It was set aside during Brecht's visit to Berlin, but was still on the agenda when he finally moved there in 1924, when it was re-jigged and put in a Kiplingesque Anglo-Indian setting to become the comedy *Man equals Man*. Of the other unfinished projects mentioned, however, not much survives. *David*, which certainly sounds the most interesting, consists of three (handwritten) scenes and a number of plans and ideas. *Summer Symphony* (or *Hanne*), which was reputedly almost finished by the end of 1919, has disappeared apart from a handful of notes. *Malvi* (5 September 1920) seems to have got nowhere, *Pope Joan* little further, though there is an interesting résumé of the story showing Joan as a strong, stocky peasant girl who looks as if her face 'was made of earth' and is good at 'facts, sums, power and cynicism'. All that exists of *The Fleshboat*, the 'operetta' mentioned on p. 4, is the bare notion of a storm-tossed sailing ship containing '4 niggers, 1 white man and a mulatto woman fleeing from the plague', all of them drunk and noisy, with a boy up the mast as a kind of narrator; at the end the white man, who has a club foot, auctions off the ship and its passengers. But what Brecht's references to such schemes do suggest is a good deal about his methods of working at this stage of his life: the way in which an idea would germinate, normally as a story and a setting, less often as a central figure, then throw off a few first shoots in the form of passages of dialogue which might be worked up later into coherent scenes or else left to wither away. They can be seen in relation to his poems and to the other plays or film stories which he was thinking about, as also to his private concerns. The film stories themselves, for instance, clearly relate to his need to earn money quickly for his planned life with Marianne. Neither then nor twenty years later in Los Angeles does he seem to have been drawn to the film medium for its own sake.

For anyone interested in Brecht's poems the diary entries are extremely instructive. For we see not only when some of them were written, but also what some of their references mean. Thus, besides the 'Ballad of the Love-Death', whose physical setting and poetic language can be seen to lie very close to the 1922 version of *In the Jungle* with its almost symbolist use of atmospheric colour, the poem 'An Inscription Touches Off Sentimental Memories' springs directly from Brecht's reading of an old letter on 9 October 1921. A number of the poems actually included in the diary, moreover, figure neither in the English-language selection nor even in the collected German edition. It is also possible to gather something of his various plans for grouping and collecting his poems prior to the compilation of *Devotions for the Home* (*Hauspostille*) in the course of 1922. The 'lute primer' which he envisages publishing (31 August 1920) is presumably much the same as the *Guitar Primer* or *Songs to the Guitar by Bert Brecht and His Friends* which was apparently his earliest collection, complete with home-made tunes. The 'Psalms' too are already an entity, of a very different kind, and virtually complete by the time the diary starts; a late example occurs in the entry for 29 May 1921. It is also interesting that he should have thought of writing a book of

'Visions'; there are various poems and short prose pieces of different dates to which he gave this heading, and others which seem to fall under it, though for a long time they were not seen in relation to one another. All three of these schemes antedate anything that appeared in Brecht's lifetime, and until the publication of his collected works in the 1960s the poems of which they are composed remained unknown.

At the same time this book is a rich source of clues to the literary influences which affected both plays and poems, as also about the whole mixture of ingredients which went to make up the peculiar world of Brecht's imagination. So we find him already reading Kipling and Upton Sinclair and coming for the first time on Chesterton's Father Brown detective stories, which he sees as evidence of English practicality: problems to be solved by rational means. Probably he read such authors in translation at this stage, but this does not stop him from dropping in the odd Anglo-Saxon term: 'allright' [*sic*] for instance, or 'That's all', which for some reason becomes the nickname for his slightly mephistophelean Augsburg friend Orge (George) Pfanzelt. Already, too, he admires Alfred Döblin, the former Expressionist who later became a friend and ally in the promotion of the 'epic theatre'. Along with these, however, and with the well-known example of Rimbaud, he appreciates such comparatively unexpected writers as Hamsun, Tagore and the French novelist Charles-Louis Philippe, while Hebbel seems to be the established German literary figure who means most to him. In mid-June 1921 he sees Georg Kaiser's *From Morn to Midnight*, a famous Expressionist play by one of the few contemporary playwrights he has much use for, starring Alexander Granach, an actor later to be closely associated with his own work. Then in Wiesbaden he sees what may well be his first Charlie Chaplin film: one that made a deep enough impression on him for him to recall it in a poem nearly a quarter of a century later. Whether for commercial or for administrative reasons, the Chaplin films were not allowed to enter Germany until that year, but from that point on they helped to determine Brecht's ideas of externalised, non-'psychological', behaviouristic acting.

The world which he was thus forming for himself was a strange pot-pourri of classical, biblical and wildly exotic elements, to be seen at its most impressive perhaps in his vivid yet basic, down-to-earth version of the David story. At this stage it is still the exotic side that seems to predominate, whether the imagery is that of the Far East, the Western frontier with its braves and wigwams, or the South American pampas. So the references to Asia, Malaya, Tahiti fuse in a single mythology which relates *In the Jungle* – first of Brecht's many exotic plays – to the obsessive appeal of Marianne Zoff. With her broad face, combed-back hair and brown skin she becomes the Maori woman, the squaw, the Gauguin girl from Tahiti, to be taken into the Kraal (an Afrikaans term) or sought in absurdly remote places: the Himalayas perhaps, or Timbuctoo. Coy as this private language often seems, and absurdly at variance with Brecht's more hard-headed insights into the impossibility of their relationship, it is close to that of the Shlink-Garga conflict in his equally mythical Chicago, where Shlink for unexplained reasons is a Malay, Garga hopes to get away to Tahiti, and there is a Chinese Hotel where Shlink keeps Garga's sister and reminisces about his youth on the Yangtse-kiang. By such means Brecht arrived at what he later termed a 'poetic conception': that is, an imaginary setting for dramatic action such as he also found in the Indian garrison town of Kilkoa (for *Man equals Man*) or the pullulating slums of Victorian London (for *The Threepenny Opera* in 1928). Such creations could be justified in terms of his later doctrine of 'alienation', according to which the strangeness of the setting helps us to see the actual events in a more critical light. None the less it seems clear that they also have a quite personal, sensual element, which he enjoyed for its own sake.

And yet something of the 'alienation' theory is already there, as in his realisation, while lying in hospital in Berlin, that *Baal* and *In the Jungle* both had the merit of not attempting to carry their audience away: 'Instinctively I've kept my distance'. He is still some way from trying to work out a consistent theoretical or philosophical position; aware, no doubt, of his own inconsistency he complains early on that he cannot remember what opinions he has held, then goes on to warn himself against the danger of having only one theory instead of finding riches for himself in between the many theories available. At the same time he is aware that his gift is for the concrete and tangible, asking himself why he cannot write about what he loves in Marianne: 'one only sees the objective facts; feelings are too strong'. And because of the shrewd and sceptical vision which this gives him he notes down a number of original and revealing perceptions: about the invidiousness of comparisons, for instance, ('characteristics should take off their hats to one another, instead of spitting in each other's faces'), or, more surprisingly, the limitations of the 'binary' outlook where everything is described in terms of pairs of opposites. With this he is striking at the root of German polarised thinking, and thereby of the thesis–antithesis language of the dialectic which was later to become so important to him. It is not that he is 'undialectical' or refuses to admit how situations develop from a tangle of conflicting elements; but he mistrusts the simplifications needed to make such issues intelligible to 'sparrow-sized brains'.

Underlying the subsequent theoretician, then, we see that there is a pragmatist, and when the latter eventually in the 1950s began to check (and even slightly to mock) the former it was not such a surprising development after all. Certainly it is he who, in the present volume, provides the sharpest insights, ruthless, down to earth, stoical and fully worthy of a great writer. Look, for example, at his dissatisfaction with the history books to which he turns for information bearing on the Papacy around 860 A.D.; read his description of words as so many 'protective coatings', along with his vivid picture of the state of mind of his friend Pfanzelt; or take his pungently realistic yet not fundamentally hostile account of the churches' exploitation of Jesus: such passages stimulate thought and show a unique blend of scepticism and imaginative power. Perhaps the best summary of his black yet lucid philosophy at this stage is given by a note made shortly before the diary begins, prompted no doubt by his mother's sufferings:

> Whenever I have seen people wringing their hands or launching accusations as a result of pain and worry they have always struck me as quite failing to appreciate the full seriousness of their situation. For they had completely forgotten that it was all no use; they hadn't yet realised that God had not simply forsaken or offended them, but that there was actually no God whatever and that a man who causes a rumpus all by himself on a desert island must be off his head.

He still has a very striking appreciation of colourful language; now and again his pen runs away with him in a way it seldom did in later, austerer times. But how many other young writers would have the self-denial to say 'In the beginning was not the word. The word is at the end. It is the thing's dead body'? His secret was his ability to see through all the literature to the basic realities, however unpleasant. 'O God, please let my sight always cut through the crust, pierce it!' God or no God, his prayer was heard.

*

Until these diaries became accessible the main source for our knowledge of the young Brecht was Hans Otto Münsterer's delightful *Bert Brecht. Erinnerungen aus den Jahren 1917–22* (Reminiscences from the years 1917–22) which appeared in 1963 and largely dovetails with the present book. The diaries themselves are in four handwritten booklets covering the periods June–September 1920, February–May 1921, end of May–end of September 1921, and thence to the middle of February 1922, where the book ends. Only three of these come from the Brecht Archive; the second remained with Marianne Brecht, who later married the actor Theo Lingen, and was made available by her and Brecht's daughter. Between the first and second there must have been another, bridging the four-month gap, but it has never been found. Some of the entries in the three booklets in the Archive appeared earlier in the section of Brecht's Collected Works devoted to his theoretical writings on literature and art, *Schriften zur Literatur und Kunst*, and have therefore been drawn on for the editorial apparatus to the Random House and Eyre Methuen editions of Brecht's plays. Those poems, too, that are included in the diaries are some of them also in the Eyre Methuen volume *Poems 1913–1956*, and where this is so the same translations are used. Explanatory notes will be found throughout the text; they are largely based on those of the German editor Herta Ramthun, but have been both shortened and supplemented for American and British readers. In addition there is at the back of the book a Dramatis Personae covering the main characters in the story: Brecht's family and his closest Augsburg and Munich friends, along with one or two others who demand more than a short footnote. Both then and later Brecht relied a great deal on such people to stimulate him and allow him to test his ideas. Their personalities and backgrounds

and their different relationships with him are therefore of some
relevance to the evolution of his work.

Though there are also a number of isolated autobiographical
notes scattered among his papers between spring 1922, when the
present diary ends, and the start of his mature 'Working Journal' in
July 1938, we have chosen to confine the present book to the
period covered by the diaries proper. Later of course he was to
develop into a succession of somewhat different and far more
familiar figures: the destructively cynical *enfant terrible* of *The
Threepenny Opera*, the austerely didactic Communist of the years
around 1930, the largely isolated refugee of the wonderfully fruitful
Scandinavian period, the awkward guest in California and New
York, finally the sage of East Berlin. It seemed best not to get
involved with these but to leave the twenty-four year old Brecht a
little short of the first great changes in his life: the Munich
production of *Drums in the Night*, the award of the Kleist Prize, the
(doomed) marriage to Marianne Zoff, the appointment as
dramaturg to the Kammerspiele. Already he was able to take stock
of himself, to decide to drive himself in the direction he wanted;
between the lines a good deal of self-discipline can be inferred.
Already he was a mixture of contradictions, the hot heart in a cold,
shy, detached person. Already he foresaw the fearful precarious-
ness of 1920s Berlin, 'one's utter abandonment to infinitesimal
differences of calculation, payment, luck'. Shining through
everything, however, is the evidence of his poetic and theatrical
genius: thus the old man David talks about the building of a water
conduit; Malvi dies miserably in the rain and mud;

> The trembling of a few blades of grass, which I noticed long ago
> Comes finally to an end

– as two sad-faced clowns comment on the action and pull the play
to pieces, or a baggy-trousered comic sings in mid-stage.
Whereupon 'a lot of people slope on to the stage and join in, lots of
them, in increasing numbers, filling the entire stage, wearing red
ties, and bawling out that it can't apply to them'.

The results still lie in the future. But here are some of the
ingredients out of which great theatre will be made.

J.W.

NOTE

Minor explanatory notes are given at the foot of most pages. For a number of the more important characters in the story fuller entries are given on pp. 162–169. These are the people who were particularly close or significant to Brecht, whether for personal or for professional reasons. In the order in which the entries occur, they are:

WOMEN

'Bi' Banholzer
Fanny Pfanzelt
Mrs Feuchtwanger
'He' or **Hedda** Kuhn
Sophie Brecht (**'Mama'**)
'Ma', **'Mar'** or Marianne Zoff
Marie Roecker
Rosmarie or **Rosie** Aman

MEN

Arnold **Bronnen**
Wilhelm **Brüstle**
'Cas' Neher
Berthold Brecht (**'Father'**)
Lion **Feuchtwanger**
Frank Banholzer
Alexander **Granach**
Rudolf **Hartmann**
Heinrich Eduard Jacob
Hermann **Kasack**
Klabund
'Lud' Prestel
'Orge' or **George** Pfanzelt
Otto Müllereisert
Recht
Walter Brecht
Frank **Warschauer**
Otto **Zarek**
Otto **Zoff**

The names or nicknames under which they are to be found are emphasised by **heavy type** on their first appearance in the main text.

J.W.

Bertolt Brecht: Diaries 1920–1922

Edited by HERTA RAMTHUN

Translated and annotated by JOHN WILLETT

Mid-June to end of September 1920.

JUNE

Tuesday 15th.

Not a breath of wind round me: I could be mending my sails. But what's the point of bothering about myself. I've got toothache and am writing a bad play – for the fourth time – and then those crushing worries about **Bi** and slow thoughts about **Mama** ...

Wednesday 16th.

Zeiss[1] doesn't want to do *Baal*,[2] supposedly because of the risk of a scandal. (So why couldn't he put on a private performance?) Gutherz[3] sent for me and got rid of me in the corridor. All right, he may be too busy, but I'm no door-to-door salesman. So it's goodbye to this winter's great sensation.

Thursday 17th.

Cas is doing designs for a church, based on an idea of mine. An altarpiece: a miserable-looking man, dressed just in a pair of trousers, being escorted up to heaven by angels. A ceiling painting (4 × 6m.): great swarms of people flying towards the light. What Cas has done so far is first rate, rather in the style of Greco, for whom he currently has a passion. He is always reading Plutarch 'because he gives you a sense of elegance'.

Friday 18th.

How this Germany bores me! It's a good middling country, with lovely pale colours and wide landscapes: but what inhabitants! A degraded peasantry whose crudeness however doesn't give birth to any fabulous monsters, just a quiet decline into the animal kingdom; a middle class run to fat; and drab intellectuals. The answer: America ...

Sunday 20th.

Bi is losing weight and her breast is prickling. Dr. Renner[4] says there is the start of something top left, but the Banholzers shrug

[1] Carl Zeiss, 1871–1924. Director-general of Bavarian State Theatres from 1920 until his death.

[2] Brecht's first play, submitted the previous summer.

[3] Gerhard Gutherz, 1877–1942, chief dramaturg of the Residenz-Theater in Munich from 1915–35.

[4] Dr Renner had been Brecht's mother's doctor.

their shoulders, refuse to have her X-rayed, and want her to get a job instead. What a family. For the past year all my Sundays have been given up to Bi.

Monday 21st to Saturday 26th.
I've been lounging around on the sofa and playing the guitar. Lots of thoughts, but the flesh is weak and nobody's strong enough to get me going. Then I've been to tea with **Hedda**, who has been remote from me for some months now, like the usual whirlpool that forms round a hole, an empty place. One evening Anni Bauer came to the studio, we drank schnaps under the lantern, I twanged the guitar, kissed her, started to get cheeky, but she smelt to me like a poor girl so I sent her home. What's more I'm scared of Go[norrhea]. I'm getting more ideas than last winter. I might write a book of *Visions*, or heavenly farces (à la Greco), or a comic sketch for Valentin[5] (preposterous) – and the upshot is that I'm writing damn all. Damn all is invariably the best thing anybody could write. In my free time I've been reading Plutarch on Sulla and Maurice Barrès on El Greco, the sort of book I like, strong and delicate. Am much affected by it, particularly the (left-hand) angel in *The Assumption of the Blessed Virgin*, the one that's telling her something serious as she flies upwards, it's quite amazingly beautiful. At the end of the week I heard a reading by E. Lasker-Schüler,[6] good and bad poems, exaggerated and unhealthy, but extremely beautiful in parts. The woman herself is old and worn out, flabby and unappealing. Then later on I went for a walk in the Englischer Garten[7] with Hedda and understood a lot, had my hands full of dandruff and told her I didn't love her, but Bi and **George**: that it's not a question of activity but of repose etc. In the course of all this I sketched out an operetta with words, *The Fleshboat*, also a piece on the comedian Karl Valentin.

Sunday 27th.
Now and again my work strikes me as being maybe too primitive and old-fashioned, or else crude and lacking in boldness. I hunt around for new forms and experiment with my feelings just like the

[5] Karl Valentin, the great Munich clown.
[6] Else Lasker-Schüler, 1869–1945, poet associated with Expressionism.
[7] The main Munich public park.

very latest writers. But then I keep coming back to the fact that the essence of art is simplicity, grandeur and sensitivity, and that of its form coolness. (I realise I haven't expressed that very well.)

Three of us spent the afternoon and evening at **Otto**'s: an unknown girl called Hilde Münch, Bi and myself. Bi made pancakes and had her photograph taken in her kimono. Afterwards we sat for a while in the cathedral square; she was very tired and had a temperature: I begged and begged her not to go off to her job until Monday when the results of her lung examination would have arrived. She assured me she intended to wait, so we said goodbye.

I can never work properly in the summer. I can't keep glued to my chair. What's more I am too one-sidedly positive. So now I'm being held up from getting on with *Galgei*[8] and *Hanne*[9] by their prevalent negative tendency. *Galgei* went much better so long as Ligarch and his Shindy Club were my trump card.

Monday 28th and Tuesday 29th.
To the Starnberger See[10](Pöcking) with Cas, Hedda and Edith Blass.[11] The whole day swimming from a boat. Hedda swam like an otter and the lake made Cas stagger with sheer pleasure although it was raining when he first saw it. On the second evening we returned home dog-tired, with almighty sunburns but in excellent heart. Full of sun and water and not un-smelly.

Wednesday 30th.
Augsburg in the afternoon, Bi having decided to make the trip. I saw her X-ray: there is indeed something wrong with her lung. What's more she had developed a temperature. I managed to persuade her to stay at home. Returned exhausted in the evening.

---

[8] Unfinished play which later developed into *Man equals Man*. Ligarch and the Shindy Club figure in it.

[9] Name of a character in the fragmentary play *Sommersinfonie*.

[10] Lake seventeen miles south-west of Munich. Pöcking is a village near it.

[11] Edith Blass. Friend of Cas Neher.

JULY

Thursday 1st.
I've gradually got back to work on *Galgei*. I'm full of ideas. For a
play about Jesus, for a play about Bi. Am also full of fresh insights
as to how one might write novels that would grip the reader by
taking the existing tradition, as created by (all other) novels, and
judicially killing it off. We've already reached a stage where it's
impossible to give a compelling description of death because every
conceivable way of dying has already been rehearsed and all one
can do is borrow. As soon as an action is portrayed in a particular
style this creates a particular mood that manages to even out the
reader's emotional fluctuations; what's more, anything that's
portrayed then seems to have (not only been seen or portrayed but
also) occurred and been experienced from one single point of view.
But what stylistic possibility is there that might let one make use of
this awareness? E.g. should the principal character's death perhaps
be depicted in a new style, maybe journalese? That's impossibly
awkward. Another point: there are three ways of arriving at a
grand conspectus. (1) You can make your principal conflict out of
the clash between simple inner life and outer incidentals
('politics'). (2) You can confine yourself to portraying the inner
life, isolated and detached, hard, un-atmospheric, subversive and
yet acquiescent. (3) You can prove that the inner life (and major
conflicts) doesn't exist, and furnish the externals. Of these (1) is a
job for the journalist. It's difficult not to take sides. Even if one
managed to represent the hero as *un*demanding, it would still look
as though one considered human beings to be something
excessively valuable, constricted only by unfavourable circumstances and so forth. But after all it is they themselves who create
the circumstances, or else they just die an accidental death, get
murdered by other people. (2) is the toughest nut to crack. If one
leaves out everything external and goes to work naked, then
formidable structural qualities or superhuman strength are needed
to compensate. This is where one runs most risks from the
linguistic point of view: i.e. the risk of routine or of idolatrous
word-worship.

Sunday 4th.
Bi. The Orchideengarten.[12] She said some marvellous things: 'But I *can* swim. Only twice, though. Then I shall get so tired I'll die.'

Orge, hoarse-voiced and transparent, is trying for his exam. Otto has finished his finals, he manages everything without any effort. Life to him is a kind of sport, and all he does is 'dodge everything'.

Tuesday 6th.
I keep getting insights into the true nature of great art. I used to be further forward in this respect. But I'm beginning to get there once more. In *Galgei* what needs to be brought out is the element of eternity, simplicity: in the year of Our Lord ... citizen Joseph Galgei fell into the hands of bad men who maltreated him, took away his name and left him lying skinless. Everyone should look to his own skin.

Been to the cinema a lot. Specially detective dramas. What I like about them is the gymnastic aspect. (The only elegant thing about Him ...) With E. Blass in the Englischer Garten in the evening. In among the scents of the lime trees I tell of 1919's drunken excesses. (Meanwhile my left eye is still on Galgei. He emerges from the crowd of – fat, colourful – creatures and stands in the middle rather stolidly, as if answering a distant summons.) **Feuchtwanger** has jabbed his glasses into his eye and has been sitting hunched in the dark in his room with a swollen face like a child's. The injured Maccabean. His display of respectful interest in *Galgei* is heartening. He is a good man and a strong one, extremely clever and decent.

Wednesday 7th.
Everything I've been writing lately has been bad and ordinary – potatoes for poor people – even though all I have been doing is to write it. Perhaps this is one of the main reasons, though. The days have been hot and sunny, tarred streets are not my kind of thing, I've a continual pressure at the back of my head. Meanwhile a lot of time is passing. I'm not making use of it. I'm simply glad when it's gone, like skin peeling after sunburn. I blame everything,

---

[12] In Augsburg. Literally 'orchid garden'.

including the size of my window, which dazzles me with the amount of light and reveals a phoney sky, distorted by glass. All I need for *Galgei* is the impetus. So far as the concept goes everything is 'allright'.[13] Now I want to stop writing, my headache's getting worse. I don't believe anything terrible happens in hell. What will happen there is *damn all*. Sauve qui peut!

If only I were a painter! They are like women: always ready for it. The notion of self-mortification by work! The smell of paint, the resistance of the material and the eternal availability of the object: all this stimulates and satisfies.

It's so quiet. If one could only calm down to the great simple rhythm of life, the eating of potatoes, the dances in little plank-lined rooms, the sad sunsets in which the air expands, the unvaried eternal conflicts without distinction or refinement. You rail against the uniformity of all life – the mute dumbwitted way in which all living creatures refuse to meet their old needs in fresh forms – because you yourself are poor and have no compelling needs.

At night, a mouthful of firewater in my stomach, I get overcome by a vast desire to do other work, to mould the simple darkness of life – tough and servile, cruel and realistic – with a *love* of life. I still have to get shot of *Galgei* and *Sommersinfonie*, but after that the Expressionist vein will be exhausted and 'expression' can be thrown on the dungheap. Expressionism represented a (little German) revolution, but as soon as a certain degree of freedom was permitted, it turned out that there were no free people around; as soon as one imagined one could say what one wanted, it turned out to be what the *new* tyrants wanted; and they had nothing to say. These striplings, while richer in words and gestures than earlier generations, displayed the whole trivial frivolity of any *jeunesse dorée*, its habit of taking its own boredom for pessimism, its irresponsibility for boldness, and its impotence and unreliability for freedom and an urge to action.

It is still a long way to the sky, but the crows are already flying over those people.

Thursday 8th.
I have been absorbing Van Gogh's letters to Theo. They are deeply

---

[13] 'allright'. Brecht writes it thus in English.

moving documents of poverty and frantic work. He paints in lieu of eating, and reckons up how much paint his tuberculosis has presented him with. He has no success but works like a maniac and practically all the time sees the future as blacker than the present, which is too black to start with. There's an enormous amount to be learned from that, and not only on the human side. It might do me quite a lot of good if I were to work that way, gloomy and bull-headed, laying no stress on inspiration, and spitting on flashy ideas. But this can only be achieved by description, one has to know a lot, have a certain amount of experience behind one and possess a particular style that can be 'applied' to anything. In any case one needs to beware of 'wit', of candied fruit, tasteful decorations and smooth finish. The overriding thing must be the greatness of the conception, the dark piled-up mass, the trembling light over everything and the fearlessness of the human heart which shows things as they are and likes them that way.

Spend the afternoon at Possenhofen[14] with E. Weiss.[15] Up to seven thunderstorms in the evening. Green meadows in a sulphurous light, dark blue trees, puddles of water like holes in the earth, split open. Somehow or other one is electrically connected with the discharges, the lightning gives one courage and tightens the skin on one's face, and the result is clarity. I love thunderstorms.

Friday 9th.
At Johst's.[16] His face looked lined. Had a success in Dresden with *Der König*. 'Did you like the play?' J: 'Yes, it was a splendid performance. Quite different from what I had imagined, of course. The opposite. Prettified. Not young and disturbing: smooth and sentimental. But that's just what made it a success.' Sitting there is a thin-lipped young gent with a coolly ironic look: Suhrkamp,[17] who has what J. calls a tidy approach to imaginative writing. 'They don't like him.'

[14] On the Starnberger See.

[15] E. Weiss. Edith Blass may be meant.

[16] Hans Johst, b. 1890, Munich Expressionist playwright. Later the President of the Reichsschrifttumskammer under the Nazis.

[17] Peter Suhrkamp, 1891–1959. Dramaturg and director at Landestheater, Darmstadt from 1921–25. Brecht's publisher after the Second World War.

Sunday 11th.
Bi is getting better. Orge is coughing like a couple of hospitals, it makes him fly round his room; one moment his stomach aches, the next moment his head, and all the time his hands are hot. But he's a great philosopher. At home all's quiet. I keep on going to the cemetery, and I like it there.

Monday 12th.
'They that hold on to much shall be laden therewith. But they that fail to give little, their hands shall wither on their arms'.

How I dislike hearing these women like Hedda and Edith telling about something that's happened. It's all wrong, dolled up and lacking in style, the sentences are like abcesses or carbuncles, inflated and with unhealthy bright colours. What's more, nothing is exactly right, and I don't care for judgements. Am also resistant to intimate confessions, don't like a fuss, feel on edge: the whole thing's phoney. Listening to Bi on the other hand is a pleasure: I know what she's like, and she doesn't embroider things.

Thursday 15th.
It's evening and I'm sitting in the studio. A certain amount of sun coming in. A white curtain fluttering in front of the big window, and a red lantern in front of that. I'm in my shirtsleeves, wearing a straw hat, my body contains tea, I'm sated. *Baal* has gone to press, and I've got all the galleys. As for human relationships, a certain amount of confusion prevails. I'm not so strong as I sometimes am, it is ebb-tide, but now it is evening and I'm glad. Perhaps I shall be able to do some powerful art again in the autumn.

Spent four hours yesterday with Feuchtwanger, who read his Italian comedy to me.[18] I liked it because I like *him*, moreover it's technically interesting and contains lovely images. Once again there's a lot of Brecht in it. The American is Kragler, that's sure. The structure of the first act depends on having this gentleman suddenly appear to everybody's surprise at the end as they are all sitting there not expecting him to turn up, then he stands in the door and just says 'Good evening'. ('The name is Kragler.')[19] The

---

[18] Feuchtwanger's 'Italian comedy' was a play called *Der Amerikaner oder Die entzauberte Stadt.*

[19] 'The name is Kragler.' Phrase from Brecht's second play, *Drums in the Night*, Kragler being its leading character.

conclusion: he messes up a tremendous (technical) achievement for the sake of a woman and starts work afresh. What's more the play is short on grandeur and significance. It has wit (but not overmuch), taste (but not enough) and technique (but not good, just slick).

Friday 16th.
Spent the afternoon at Possenhofen with Cas. It's better with a friend than with a girl. We lay in the water (77° Fahrenheit) and in the forest and then in the boat, then had another swim when night had already fallen. If you lie on your back the stars above move with you, while through you flows the current. At night you tumble into bed like a ripe fruit, voluptuously.

Sunday 18th.
In the Lech canal[20] on Saturday evening. Fireflies under forests of greenery, into which you haul yourself up out of the water. Returned there on Sunday afternoon. Orge strolled down the canal. Cas painted under a grey parasol, then we went home to tea, for which Bi joined us. After dark had an ice at the Orchideengarten, then composed a Psalm 'I know her heart is bad' while walking, then to Gabler's[21] to drink bilberry wine and read Psalms,[22] after that back with Orge.

Monday 19th to Saturday 24th.
Munich. In mid-week wrote 'Ballad on many ships',[23] followed by a fourth act to *Drums in the Night*, a final one. On Saturday morning again entirely revised the fourth act, this time not at all like with *Baal* which I now realise I completely messed up. Baal has turned to paper, gone academic, smooth, well-shaved, wearing bathing trunks and all that. Instead of becoming more earthy, carefree, outrageous, simple ... In future I shall produce nothing but flaming mud pies made of shit.

[20] The river Lech skirts Augsburg on its way north to join the Danube.
[21] Gabler's Taverne. Augsburg drinking-place frequented by Brecht and his friends. (See Ill. no. 3c.)
[22] Psalms. Cycle of poems written by Brecht in 1920. This one has not survived.
[23] 'Ballad on many ships.' See *Poems 1913–1956*, p. 50.

Sunday 25th.
Bathed in the Lech. Bi looked on.

Monday 26th.
Hamsun's *Queen Tamara*[24] is an odd book. It's like something that's been written for children (this emerges most clearly where the bad things occur, like the great ranting speeches centering on the Abbot, a splendid piece of showing-off, really childish) and it's full of the sort of thing children find fun. I don't believe H. was really trying to show the basic childishness of all those fabulous potpourris of heroic life: it never emerges how comic it is to hope to become something by means of a deed; that's not what's meant, and in so far he fails, even though there is great beauty in such innocence of mind. But look at the figure of the queen, it's magnificent, rounded and childish, a Toledo blade, supple, unbreakable, aristocratic. The Prince is extremely comic; he has to stand there cap in hand, just being the prince consort, and he doesn't like this. So he puts the cap on, please note, and then imagines something significant is bound to happen which will give people something to talk about: she, the queen, will sink into the ground or go up in flames. However, nothing of the sort in fact occurs. He has got his cap on, and she accepts this and takes him into her soft arms, and who on earth wears a cap in bed? So he can go back to being prince consort. Hamsun has a lot to teach one, and at the moment that's what matters.

Tuesday 27th.
Met **Zarek**, Bazarek. He's not as clever as I'd expected, creatively speaking he has a conceptual block. On top of that he has a damned rigid style. I sang some of my songs and he described a scene from his *David*[25] (David before Saul). Apparently it had turned sticky and he had made it work by means of plotting. I said offhand it should be done without plotting. And then I demonstrated it without that. He opened his mouth wide. It popped in, then he

[24] *Queen Tamara*, play (1903) by the Norwegian writer Kurt Hamsun, 1859–1952.
[25] *David*. Play in five acts by Otto Zarek. Brecht left notes for a play of the same title, of which the only substantial fragment remaining is the Saul–David scene written the following day.

shut it again, gulped once or twice with his Adam's apple, and swallowed. He fancied he now felt like rewriting the whole thing. 'Zo?', he said.

In the evening Hedda and I went to the cinema. Scenes at sea. Why aren't there any pirate films? One day I'll write some. Another thing: why not use the theatre to put across new fashions – for clothes etc. (and get paid for this by the fashion firms)? And print plays (books?) on newsprint complete with advertisements that would pay for the whole business? One must try to establish oneself in Germany somehow ...

Wednesday 28th.

Wrote the Saul-David scene. Good stuff in it. It works without any plotting. Saul delivers his potpourri and covers all the high and low points, and during the entire switchback ride David is sitting there cutting his nails.

Yesterday I wrote the 'Ballad of Friendship'[26] and it's good. (I shall adapt it for the movies.)

Friday 30th.

In the morning I saw **Klabund**, who looks ill and is living in Unold's[27] studio with a very blonde girl. He's going to take her to the country. In the afternoon Feuchtwanger and Zarek came to tea.

Wrote the first scene of a play *Saul and David* which I propose to do on tne side and without any previous plan, though the raw material is good.

[26] 'Ballad of Friendship.' *Poems 1913–1956*, p. 52.
[27] Max Unold, 1885–1964. Was president of the Munich Neue Sezession in the 1930s.

AUGUST

Tuesday 3rd.
I've rewritten the beginning of Act 3 of *Drums* and the second (optional) ending to Act 4. Now the whole thing's finished, and even if it doesn't exactly storm the chillier peaks of Art its dynamism and humanity make it something better than a complete waste of time. I've done four versions of Act 4 and three of Act 5. I've now got two endings, one comic, one tragic.

Wednesday 4th.
On Sunday evening I decided to put on a clean shirt. This was because I wanted to take Bi to the station on Monday morning and say hullo to Hedda on her way through. After that I'd be able to go down to the Lech and think about myself. (I used to be more fashionable, according to Orge.) However, Hedda got out, thinking she could travel on in the evening, which wasn't the case. So she stayed; she didn't notice my face, which was far from patient, she just stayed. I walked along beside her like a stranger in my clean shirt, profoundly disappointed. I wanted to be lying in bed on my own, diagonally across it, with a newspaper and a looking-glass. Yesterday she left, and it's her bad luck that she looks no good when she has had a failure, and tears don't suit her face. She begins to look old then: water trickling out of a ruin. – But now I'm free at last and can improve myself.

This afternoon I went for a walk with **Lud** up the Lech as far as the weir, where we swam in the race and stretched ourselves in the sunshine. On the way home in the evening I was able to compose the 'Children's Song about Bread'[28] and a few other children's songs. That was a good start.

Thursday 5th.
Went off to charge my batteries in the hot sun. Had an idea for the *Sinfonie* ('In the red summer the lecherous butterflies ...') Red, burning images, mud and turds, shovelled together, on a small stage, hot and insolent.

---

[28] 'Children's Song about Bread'. Early version of 'The Bread and the Children', *Poems 1913–1956*, p. 60.

Saturday 7th.
Cas and I paid an early visit to Bi in Ziemetshausen.[29] She doesn't
look too well, chases around too much, is living with a gym
mistress, an adhesive creature who drags her along with her. We lie
in the brushwood and practise cinema. It's lovely to see the way Bi
acts: utterly human, utterly simple. A queen is a queen, terror is
terror, and Bi is Bi. She's got style, but she never achieves the same
effects as Nature. (When she points to the undergrowth with both
hands and exclaims delightedly 'Look at that butterfly'.) She
doesn't imitate nature, she acts. (I'm planning a film in the style of
Lendecke.)[30]

Tuesday 9th to Saturday 15th.
In Württemberg with Cas and Otto. Ehingen. Untermarchtal.
Beuron. Möhringen.[31]. On the Thursday Cas dropped out and
sailed home. We bathed every day and didn't do too much
walking. Priests gave us bread for five marks, the peasants home-
made wines. Potatoes we stole.

Tuesday 17th.
I've read Shakespeare's *Antony & Cleopatra*, a splendid drama
which really gripped me. The more central the place apparently
taken by the plot, the richer and more powerful are the
developments open to its exponents. They haven't got faces, they
only have voices, they don't keep speaking, they just answer, they
don't wear the plot like a rubber skin but wrap it round themselves
like a broad garment full of folds. When the plot is a strong one
these men needn't be walking museums, one doesn't have to make
a meal of *them*, there's also the play itself. The medium which links
audience and stage is the urge to see. The clearer the details of a
character, the thinner the connection with the observer. I love this
play and the people in it.
   In the evening I had a look at Hebbel's poems.[32] There are some
marvellous things there (as well as silly ones). How profound his

[29] Ziemetshausen. Some fifteen miles west of Augsburg.
[30] O. F. C. Lendecke, 1886–1918, a fashion artist.
[31] The places named lie in the Danube valley above Ulm.
[32] Hebbel. German poet and dramatist, 1813–63.

awareness was, and how pure and daring his poetic will! Much of this is very German (autumnal, cool, deep, flat).

Wednesday 18th.
A letter from He[dda]. I behaved badly to her last time (when I had the clean shirt on) and on many earlier occasions too; she made things devilish difficult for me and I wrestled with the devil and frequently lost. But now she has rolled up her sleeves in order to rip me to shreds with a vengeance. I'm sorry for her, she's barking at the moon, I can't hear her reproaches, at the moment I'm away in remotest India, have left my dictionary behind, she's getting hoarse, the moon is shining. It's two years now since she first made tea for me, she had much pleasure, she had much pain; she could have gone off, with wind and limb intact, she could have fought back with tooth and nail, she had a lot of worry, she had a lot of enjoyment, she had nails on her fingers and she could have gone off even in her vest. But now she's killing me. I'm to be made into mincemeat. Mincemeat turns her stomach. And I, after tiring of her when she lay limply in my bed crying ('I can't stand that noise, don't cry'), – now I can feel a fresh wind blowing: it's moving my ship along but not away; I sit down and write to her, for she's miserable and I didn't treat her well; and finally she is attacking me and I'm defending myself as best I can and remembering what I can be sorry for and behaving towards her like when she was at her best, and defending myself. That was yesterday, and the letter went off the same evening, and now I've got her second, the first one's twin, a nasty little piece of paper. 'Why didn't I have the strength at the time to break away from somebody who not only didn't love me but was crude and tactless too?' Why didn't she? Why did she merely have the strength to vomit up paper and bombard islands? I deserved it. I bow to the storm, the seas incarnadine will wash me clean, I lied, rip out my tongue! She has gone mad with rage; she is going up the wall (? to heaven), the mincemeat will be thrown to the dogs ... I am worse than nothing at all; if only she had never met me, she's sticking her finger down her throat. The dogs expire from the mincemeat ...

It's heaven's duty to take a shovel and beat me now and again as a reward for being so prone to lies and vanity. Whenever I get the least doubt about Bi's innocence it hits me in the guts, and the flies plague me till I could envy Job. But when He[dda] starts squirming high and low because I lured her out of her shell and then left her lying naked, then I remain cool as a cattle-dealer. Frequently she behaved wantonly, as Orge puts it, but I've behaved as crudely and toughly as a bull's scrotum. I should be hit with a shovel.

Since Cas stopped living on field postcards he has had consumption. He served three years in the war, yet he's too much of a coward to ask an old man for some cider, and too much of a coward to admit it, and such a liar that you'd think we had a big stick waiting for honest little boys. He lost his watch and instantly said 'I'm going back home right away'. I kept a straight face and said 'Just as well you didn't lose it in Argentina'. C: 'That's where one stops losing things.' Me: 'It can happen to anybody, even me.' C: 'People like that won't do for Argentina. I'm staying at home.' Otto and I were practically crying into the rushes. Or when we were standing in a small cemetery outside a presbytery. We wanted our supper and Cas was supposed to paint a portrait in exchange. I was going to go in, when Cas said: 'There'll have to be a bed for the night as part of this deal. Or else I just shan't start.' So I said 'go in yourself, Cas'. And he said 'right, why not?' and set off towards the door. He strode out firmly, then wheeled round to the right and careered into the church like a bullock. There we found a heap of misery in the furthest pew. Etc., etc., Finally we got fed up with him because he put pressure on us saying 'Let's chuck the money away, split up and beg our way home'. Then he ran off. He'll eat and drink the results of begging, but he doesn't like to beg himself. It's beneath him. There are times when he looks like a bumfucker.

Thursday 19th.
   She turned her back toward me
   A great fat worm appeared
   (He wanted to reward me
   And stood up to applaud me)
   But I was simply scared.

George takes his examination in September. He sits all the time in his little room behind a drawn yellow blind rummaging among local council orders. Lies on his bed coughing and cursing. **Fanny** has gone off home, things are gradually looking up for George. She was no good at all for him. In order not to lose her he tolerated B.T.'s[33] monstrous behaviour for months with an amiable smile, and now he'd like to make up for it. Previously he would never kowtow to a pig for the sake of its bacon, nor kill it because it wasn't a stallion. But now he wants to construct brilliantly ingenious catapults with which to crush this sandflea at long range. At Kimratshofen he behaved badly to Bi, worse than ever I did to Fanny, and he's so vain that he bears Bi a lasting grudge for it, also for the fact that she once failed to greet him when he was with Fanny, and on one occasion laughed. And often it seems that all he wants to do is to become secretary to some council and take Fanny home with him, as against the old days when he wanted to become nothing, and a good thing too. What's more he is acting as protector and spiritual pastor to those young creatures whom Heigei[34] has been through, and is said to have no words too bad for him. (But doesn't screw.)

Friday 20th.
I can manage to fit in the young David at some point (*David Amid the Eagles*) and write a kind of history, with no relevance, no point to the story, no 'idea', just the young David and a slice of his life. Then instead of a single interpretation there'll be hundreds and I won't have to distort anything. Moreover I'm sure that if the visions are really vivid it will acquire some element if not of reason at any rate of soul without my having to do anything about it.

I wrote the first scene right through and started the second. As for the whole, I've barely sketched out a scheme of scenes. This evening it seemed the danger was that I might slide off in the direction of grotesqueness. I must make it more concentrated and provide blood and shit rather than intellectual stuff.

To the cinema with Orge in the evening. What he likes is seeing how the four wheels of a vehicle turn; or how water flows round a corner ... He'd like (one day) to make monograms. Watercolour for the vowels. The consonants can only be represented in line, that goes without saying. Now and then he makes little drawings

---

33 B.T. Not identified.
34 Heilgei or Heigei. Otto Müllereisert.

like 'Rainy day' or 'The sceptic'. They are dadaist, with small powerful elements. Big things are always dubious. They can't be properly seen in terms of feeling. You can never smell the big things. He loves the little sentences which have eyes for this. And they bleed if pricked. His face is pale with strong bones, his forehead curiously widened out, almost brutal and slightly flattened, there's something tough and vicious there; his lips are full and handsome, like a connoisseur's, rather voluptuous; his neck short and powerful. He looks like a prelate. He told me I was getting vain, and that's not far wrong, it's the sort of thing he can spot. But I'll have to turn my guts inside out, and my skin. Let them see what I'm like inside. My thoughts are still being thought by my head alone. I must use my hands too. Being a society showpiece stinks, but it's better than being simple-minded. Still, I undertake to improve.

Saturday 21st.
I've been reading Hebbel's diaries, they are continually absorbing even if the settings are too elaborate and the feelings over-produced. Their sense of duty revolts me, likewise their idea of order, which amounts to a vast self-deception: at bottom Hebbel is a collector. He displays a restricted teleology in all his thought processes, so it seems: it is his vanity to be able to discover a meaning in anything when stupider people no longer manage to find one: nor is it common for those who have got on a long way to be brought to the point of wanting to get on even further. But there aren't all that many things that really have a meaning in Hebbel's sense. A lot are simply there, and their effects in some measure supported or denigrated. This even enters into his characters' relationships. By means of his scholastic dialectics he nearly always arrives at the most extreme possible formulation of mutual rights and duties. But it's still a tremendous distance from there to that motionless and ice-cold air that surrounds the highest intellectual exercises, a zone where right and duty fade away and the individual becomes isolated, filling the world, and relationships prove to be neither necessary nor possible. The road taken by Hebbel seems to me more and more like a blind alley. What grips us is not the magnificent gesture with which Fate crushes the great man, but just the man himself, whose fate merely displays him. His

fate is his opportunity. So it's not a matter of creating great dramas of principle which will show the way the world works and the habits of Fate, but straightforward plays depicting the fates of men, men who must be the real dividend of the play. For instance: it's not the play's job to show that fellows of some particular unusual makeup get it in the neck. But – how they behave when this happens, what they say and what sort of a face they make.

In the evening I went to the *Plärrer*[35] and rode on the swingboats. This is something I find utterly satisfying. It's one of the loveliest sports, a profitable way of spending an evening; you go home differently from normal, after those many lost empty evenings when you did nothing and got nothing out of it.

Sunday 22nd.

This afternoon Bi came; she made tea, which we had on an occasional table in the fine room sitting comfortably on the *chaise-longue*. Very pleasant; taking tea is a sport with a bit of soul to it. Bi has such pretty white legs, they decidedly merit a certain amount of attention. At the moment she's in charge of her home and responsible for bringing up her little brother. Each time she ticks him off she has to turn round in a hurry and leave the room so as not to laugh.

Before that I went for a walk with **Rosmarie**, she has bloomed and faded. I'm through with her, God help her. She remains childish, infantile, laughs a lot in an uneasy kind of way, her laugh is every bit as disturbing as a haemorrhage.

Am reading H. Hesse's *Klingsor's Last Summer*.[36] It's a very beautiful novella, slightly reminiscent of Edschmid[37] but much better. However, it's not up to the standard of *Camenzind* which I seem to remember as something cool; paper covered with a mixture of astringency and colour. One of the characters ends up just drinking red wine and going to pieces and observing the passage of the seasons and letting the moon rise: that's how he spends his time ...

[35] *Plärrer*. Name of the twice-yearly Augsburg fair. Featured in several of Brecht's early poems. (See Ill. no. 4b.)

[36] Story by Hermann Hesse, published in 1920.

[37] Kasimir Edschmid, 1890–1966. Expressionist prose writer, then living in Darmstadt.

Monday 23rd.
I have been dictating *Drums in the Night*. The third act is good apart
from one or two details. The fourth is a bastard, an abortion, a
plant a cow has squashed. This evening went on the swingboats.
Can't get *David* out of my head.

Tuesday 24th.
Munich. Feuchtwanger thinks I should leave the last scene as it is,
but the whole thing (*Baal*) read much better in manuscript. He's
right: it stinketh. One oughtn't to mind about it so much. It should
be fitted out complete with guts, heart, blood and lungs and sent
on its way with a kick up the backside. To hell with the page
proofs.

I don't think I could ever have so thoroughly developed a
philosophy as Goethe or Hebbel, who must have had memories
like tram-conductors where their own ideas were concerned. I'm
continually forgetting my opinions, can't ever make up my mind
to learn them off by heart. In the same way towns, adventures, faces
disappear in the folds of my brain quicker than the life of grass.
What shall I do when I'm old, what a miserable existence I'll lead
with my decimated past and my battered ideas like so many
arrogant cripples.

I keep on spending my evenings mooching round the *Plärrer*,
where they hammer their nigger-minstrel tunes into you till you
can't get them out of the creases of your skin at night. The month's
been slowly degenerating while we were playing at Onward
Christian Soldiers[38] in the bushes, it has taken to raining, we must
look around for fresh ways of filling our time. Films and ballad-
singing will see us through another half-moon, but after that we'll
have to take off in some other direction; lizards among the autumn
foliage in October, then huge blackbirds above the Himalayan
mountains of winter!

Wednesday 25th.
The rain rinses the last thoughts from one's head. Thoughts are
impurities. That's why they start up in the winter. Paper has lost its

[38] Onward Christian Soldiers. Literally 'Alleluia singers', perhaps in allusion to
the Salvation Army.

power to stimulate me. I hang like a bat in the turret of idleness: mouth downwards.

Thursday 26th.
There are days that are non-stop king rats of Mondays, starting at 7 a.m. Every hour another Monday starts – at 7 a.m. Monday has a special voice: it's the rattle of the alarum clock, like iron pellets being shaken up in a tin, or a dental technician drilling. On such days it's this voice that is always in your throat; on top of which the rain keeps pelting into your body through your skin, it's such a rotten skin, it's full of holes, it was a bad buy, and the worst of it is that you can't lay your hands on a curse, the curse is playing hide-and-seek, you hunt for it with your tongue but it has crawled into a hollow tooth and is gently raising hell. On such Mondays your epidermis lies asleep, fat and snoring. Suppose you could feel all this physically, its smell in your nose, its taste on your tongue, then it would be bearable, you could even make jokes about it. But there's nothing tangible, you sense it rather than feel it: so it is painful. On such days your blood never circulates right down to your fingertips, only as far as your wrists, and you'd like to eat your own tongue; except that you have to cart it around with you. On such days people behave so you'd like to let the water out of them. But without water they can't live. God has diluted them, and there's nothing to be done about it.

A charming twilight tale this evening.

I had told **Rosie** to come. She shuffled up around seven o'clock, it was just starting to get dark. Delicately she insinuated herself, she had no hat on, her neat narrow forehead was always her best asset. She made a better impression than on Sunday. We walked to the Birkenau.[39] We slithered about on a bench, she was pale, childlike, lascivious. The sky was clouded, it swam away over our heads while the wind made a noise among the bushes; groping under their foliage I regret to say. I gave her soft little face a good kissing and squashed her a bit. Apart from that she believes in doing the proper thing in every conceivable situation and has to be home at 9. But she has a lot of charm, and she's not quite as talkative as she used to be: still a big baby, thank heaven ...

[39] Birkenau. Literally 'birch meadow'.

Tonight, trotting like a cold beast through clustering undergrowth – the clouds come down virtually on the back of your head – I once again tackled *Galgei*. The brutal necessity that shoves Ligarch's hat down over his ears and strips Galgei's skin off him, the element of fluctuation and uniqueness, the evil plot and the great creatures around the little nightlight, acting as a lure despite all – if only the poetic idea could remain virginal once the disgusting business of defloration has been got over . . .

I've also started to write ballads for the boys.[40] 'The battle among the treestumps' and 'Goger Gog the toy soldier'. Also one or two things in the cynical manner of the early guitar songs, because the repertoire is exhausted and verse after verse sucked so dry that you have to masticate with your jaws when you take them in your mouth. Once again I've developed an appetite for songs about tramps, the kind that need to be cold, plastic and unflinching, that knock out one or two of the listener's teeth like tough nutshells once he gets them between his dentures.

When Georgie and Buschiri and their friend go on the town
With their flippers in the pockets, on their lips a cigarette
They can see old people standing in the doorway on their own
Who aren't blind or hard of hearing and aren't quite decrepit
    yet.
        And these comment with some loathing
        On Buschiri's dapper clothing
        On Georgie's billiard craze
        And their friend who also plays.

When Georgie and Buschiri and their friend lie in the hay
With their hand up some girl's knickers and their mind no
    doubt on God
They will see among the bushes some old boy who's had his
    day
With no apples, with no foliage, with no rod . . .
        Who will gossip on for ages
        About Buschiri's fear of babies
        And Georgie's spinal scar
        And their friend, who's worse by far.

[40] Nothing can be identified under the titles given, though the name Gogher Gogh survived as that of the gangster in Brecht's last play *Turandot*.

When Georgie and Buschiri and their friend get pissed one
   sees
How they loosely hug each other, with a table overhead.
After washing in the river and then drying in the breeze
Once more they're fresh as daisies back in bed.
> But the old get even sicker
> At Buschiri's debts for liquor
> And poor Georgie's downhill trend
> To say nothing of their friend . . .

When Georgie and Buschiri and their friend in turn get old
They'll use jacks to force their hats on, as their heads will be so
   big.
Drunken hymns will find them deaf then, pretty clothes will
   leave them cold.
For girls' hair and breasts they will not give a fig.
> Toothless they'll sit there musing
> On billiards, clothes and boozing
> Spinal scars and drifting down
> And those nights out on the town.[41]

Friday 27th.
What distinguishes those of my works which have grown from
those which have been manufactured is their deadly seriousness.
Otherwise I put in too much irony, and this makes the characters
too genial: I don't allow them any nasty motives. I underestimate
them. That way lies comedy and operetta. It's all right for people to
be comic in the higher sense while being serious, capable or
repulsive when seen close to; nor is there any reason why they
should not have comic characteristics so long as these are
important. Or again so long as the writer's landscape, language
and philosophy have a comic content.

   I am much taken up with the fate of a man who escapes to South
America in his forties in order to do something for himself, and
then gets it in the neck. Here is a man. He is tough and nasty, he
fights for his own advantage tooth and nail, he hates his family but

---

[41] This poem (about Pfanzelt, Müllereisert and Brecht) is not in the German
collected edition of 1967.

exploits it none the less, he is lazy even though it bores him. It is all shown 'as you go in', with a fat finger, mercilessly: Here is the kind of man he is. But then he falls beneath the wheels, neck downwards, into the strong black mud that's crammed into his mouth, down his throat; he learns to crawl and suffer, with his mouth shut – and in spite of it all they let him die wretchedly, they don't bother about him. There isn't a woman in the world he can rely on, nor is there a man in the world (including himself). In the end he goes blind, he skids about on his knees, he gets water on the knee, no-one washes him, there's a keg of spirits there for him, it gets taken away, brought back again, they tell him 'Someone's pissed in it.' He howls like a dog, a dog in the dark who doesn't even get beaten any longer. The sense of it all is that he realises who he is and what belongs to him (what hurts him belongs to him), even though it ends up differently with him having to die on his own, abandoned by himself. He tells all those standing round him: 'Learn how to curse, run to the sailors' dives, run your feet off, write it all down on paper, learn those curses by heart, so that you've got them when your skins are about to be stripped off, so that you've got names for everything and fists with which to start hammering against it!'

'Oh, now I know myself, get out, Par Chem,[42] heavy rain, I know God threw me into the battle, after which he was free to lie down and go to sleep. (He stretches out his hands.) There's music under my skin like a snoring walrus, I'm not desperate any longer. 10 000 devils are drumming at me, previously there were 9999; previously I was desperate, now I'm glad, There's a skeleton under my flesh, the piercing icy wind tells me, I never knew. I announce that I'm for it, get out, Par Chem! How calm it all is, the way the stores are, and the trees notice nothing, and I suppose you're laughing now. But I'm being almost ripped out of the ground, I feel the tempest so strongly, though you don't, you thick-skinned black mammy, go away, I spit in the direction of your smell of full stomach and rotten thighs and 700 brats who eat earth and feel nothing. Does God always have to use such a tempest on me? Oh, it shows me that I am something, a tiny grain, a drum, a flea-particle. Everything is subdued and thick-flowing, and the air

---

[42] Par Chem. Significance unknown.

round me is like brackish water. I am the little grain of salt that makes it bitterer. Just go away, all of you!'

Saturday 28th.
Early in the morning there was a small tragi-comedy on the stairway. Women screaming, a dog crying. Then a whistle from my father in his nightshirt. I rush to the window. The first thing I see is faces at the windows over the way. The second, two dogs in the middle of the street with their backsides coupled together. They'd be glad to separate, they'd give a lot to, Ina,[43] the feminine party, whimpers. Fräulein **Marie** explains excitedly to **Father** why she can't do anything to help, can't go down; Father bellows in that case she should at least hold her tongue. Meanwhile Peppi, aged eighteen, runs down and thumps their backsides, which merely hurts. A man walking past calmly tells her 'The only answer is a bucket of water. Thumping is no good.' She fetches one. She is wearing a short red skirt, has a slim proud carriage, is equipped with heroism and humour. Ina has suddenly acquired an expression, one of helplessness and suffering; she rolls her eyes upwards in horror, she can't think what they've been doing to her. She has been on heat for some time, but has virtuously beaten off all assaults. As soon as the water splashes on their backsides, in some mysterious way their liberation occurs.

How tragicomic this creature's divinely passive urge to fulfil her duty, her self-abandonment to rape, her maidenly cries as again and again she keeps still for that great black, heavy-haired wolf!

I realise I'm weak on verbs. But verbs are the foundation of the drama. I am building up a vocabulary, watching it like the rolling balls at roulette. I must do better.

Mustn't work metaphysics into *Galgei*: it simply needs to be worked out. Just the story of a man whom they break (they have to), and the sole problem is: how long can he stand it. What reserves has he got, what marks him off, what has him by the throat? They lop off his feet, chuck away his arms, bore a hole in his head till the whole starry heaven is shining into it: is he still Galgei? It's a sex murder story.

Walking in the churchyard this evening, wrote the 'Ballad of the

---

[43] Ina. Brecht's dog, reputedly an alsatian or German shepherd.

Secrets'.[44] And tonight, between the cinema and the swingboats, the one about my mother.

Sunday 29th.

In Germany it wasn't so much the war as the war's unfavourable outcome that showed a number of people what to make of the citizen's obligations to the state. Now they are asking more for the state than ever before. And yet there's no kind of rule people find harder to bear than that of reason. They are prepared to sacrifice everything for spurious grandiose-sounding platitudes, they'll die blissfully in pig-sties if only they can be allowed to 'play a part' in the vast opera. But sensible aims are something nobody cares to die for, and even fighting for them is hampered by the possibility of death, because people think it's more sensible to live, and you can die for 'nothing' but not for something; since it would be nothing if you're dead and bereft of the deep pleasures of renunciation. In the heyday of rationalism nations had no qualms about asking their members to give up their lives.

About literature:

Masturbation is not unknown. Screwing with french letters is not unknown. But these people are masturbating with french letters.

In the afternoon Bi was there, also Otto and **Hartmann**, the chicken Biribinki. He taught us to play 'Schafskopf,[45] we sweated over the cards, Bi made tea, Otto jokes. In the evening I played billiards with Orge in the first floor rooms, Papa as usual having gone fishing. From 9.30 p.m. at the Theatercafé with Dr. **Brüstle**, who talked about Jewish girls, he being in love with one. He wasn't talking quite like that about Jews the other day, but talk is talk.

Monday 30th.

Sketched out 'Ballade von den Mitmenschen'.[46] Billiards. (It's a little table-top billiard outfit that Pa gave us for Christmas, it was

---

[44] 'Ballad of the Secrets of Any Man at All'. *Poems 1913–1956* p. 55.

[45] 'Schafskopf'. Rules are in Hoyle's book of games.

[46] 'Ballade von den Mitmenschen'. German and English texts in *Manual of Piety*.

gathering dust under our beds, we had forgotten about it, now it's having a new lease of life, spitting out dust and shaking its bandy legs.)

I'm not yet mature enough to write a novel. The first essential is maturity of the backside: to sit glued to one's chair. Great orgies of consumption have to be staged for all the senses; eyes, fingers, nose have to be fed. The main foundations however are straight-forward descriptions of events and conditions, excavating their innermost core, together with an enjoyment of objects (rather than problems). Nothing there for impatient sweet-addicts and hawkers of plots.

First thing in the morning Bi is going to Kimratshofen.

Tuesday 31st.
I've got something inside me at the moment. I'm pregnant. Perhaps it's time for me to disgorge my lute primer,[47] printed in big letters on newsprint, or in bold letters on reject paper which will disintegrate in three or four years so that the books can find their way on to the muckheap once they've been assimilated. There are some odd things in its pages, such as 'Eat Oetker's baking powder!'[48] or 'Come to Jesus now!' or 'Brecht's rhymes are best!' But it will all disintegrate; its fame may be short but its life will be shorter; a myth about these books will survive: they are mystical documents. Prefaced by a poem called 'The negroes are singing chorales above the Himalaya mountains' ...[49]

Hedda has been writing chastened letters, the revolt has been strangled at birth due to the oppressor's failure to play his part. She is crushed, she's raving about marriage, I described our relationship as something between a marriage and an adventure, a child of compromise in fact. She wants to 'be something' to one, she would like to hold court among the ancestral portraits, the Jewess of Rastatt,[50] she sings 'A little grey home in the West'[51] ...

[47] lute primer. The German text has 'Lauterbibel', here amended to 'Lautenfibel'.

[48] Oetker's baking powder. Still exists.

[49] 'The negroes are singing chorales. . .'. MS exists, but poem was omitted from German collected edition of 1967.

[50] Rastatt. Hedda Kuhn's home town.

[51] 'A little grey home in the West'. Brecht has 'Raum ist in der kleinsten Hütte', a quotation from Schiller's 'Der Jüngling am Bach'.

She has cancelled the revolt, she has decided in future to go back to quiet domestic flagellation for her entertainment.

I've been reading P. Wiegler's *Figuren*,[52] an excellent book with chiaroscuro and lots of material. Have fished out words and colours, such as swim around there in shoals. I must get back to writing *Psalms*. Finding rhymes holds one up so. Not everything needs to be singable to the guitar.

I am going to hang up sayings in my room, all over the walls, among them some indecent ones; these are good to sit under and force you to give up inviting people. As you lie on the bed feeling desperate you savour the consolation offered by these highly spiced aphorisms, and you get annoyed by them, by the banality of this existence . . .

Tonight I added a last stanza to complete 'The drunken forest sings a chorale'.[53] It's a good piece of work. To hell with being sensible! Words have their own kind of intelligence. They can be greedy, vain, crafty, pig-headed or vulgar. One should start up a Salvation Army to 'save' them, they are so degenerate. They need to be converted one by one in the sight of everybody, then forced to join the procession and be shown to the populace.

They don't want to be made too pleased with the themselves, that's the beginning of the end, it isn't the first time; they just need to be given a sense of responsibility and loaded with burdens, after which they can find their four feet and start to revive. They are not like screens put around the beds in which life is engendered. They don't serve as flunkeys to ideas but as lovers, their ironic lovers. There are also one or two that are mere impresarios. Some need to be shot, summarily, outlawed, mown down in their places: specially those that embark on mixed marriages or frequent bad company or refuse to be buried as long as they can still be the centre of attraction. Let's have law courts for words.

Billiards. The *Berliner Tageblatt* for the last two weeks, Wiegler, battle with the whore Ina, evening walk with Orge. He loves Catholicism. But the church is a kind of circus for the masses with posters on the outside advertising things that are not to be found

---

[52] *Figuren* by Paul Wiegler (1878–1949), a literary historian and journalist, appeared in 1916.
[53] 'The drunken forest sings a chorale'. Has not survived.

inside. (Similarly at fairs: outside, 'The Beheading of Louis Capet'; inside, two jugglers and some horses being flogged.) The poster says 'The Starvation Artist' or 'The Royal Skeleton' or 'Happiness for All for 11 pence' or 'I'm Not Coming Now So I'll Be Along Later' etc., etc. All they have is a book which has been handed down, and they've scribbled all over it sticking recipes and medical prescriptions on top of the wisdom. The idea was such a powerful one that when they organised it it didn't immediately collapse, just wasted gradually away. There had to be something that everyone could hear, even the deaf, even those a long way off, those in the worst seats, even those that had to be tied down to prevent them running away . . . All that stuff for a handful of fishermen vanished with the rotten Galilean who held impromptu speeches under fig trees as he looked into the still water pondering on them and the fishes. It was a handful of dates for the tongue, scarcely for the throat; and there were a thousand stomachs. The man from Galilee had had no roof over his head, they built houses for his believers, meanwhile preaching non-stop, trowel in hand, so that people didn't rush away. The man from Galilee died for himself, they called him back to life, had need of him, didn't merely quote him, sent him to his death once again, then again and again, set him up in a tabernacle, whistled to him whenever there was someone he was supposed to die for, and had him dying for killers and sceptics in round-the-clock cinema performances. It was a Sacred Action, or rather a Sacred Auction. The man of Galilee had been proud, aimless, he had seen the ruler damned for all eternity without enlightening him, he died amid a series of misunderstandings, between crooks who entered paradise alongside him, he never said what truth was, he never estimated things, never underestimated them, there they were, so that was that, he kissed Judas because he acted in character, and so he loved him. Catholicism is a system of exploitation, an American-style business complete with equality for all, promotion ladder and wage structure. Its positive element and its sense of responsibility are enough to make a bull crumple. Copernicus's discovery, which brings man closer to the beasts by taking him further from the stars, which orders man to ride his globe round and round the sun and transfers him from mid-stage to a walk-on part, is initially shot down, then proclaimed to be correct but of absolutely no consequence. 'These are very great matters which have been created that you may marvel at God; but you can live without them. Salvation depends on other things, and you don't need science to tell you where they are.' This is a piece of impertinence that cannot fail to succeed. And inside this church there are immeasurable walls deliberately left blank for people's fantasies; there's room for everything in its storerooms, all ideas can be accommodated within its dogmas. 7000 different dishes can be prepared from this plant. The pews are comfortable. The dung is used for manure. The cattle prosper. God is visibly in charge of the whole outfit. The poor man dies countless times daily for the members. The policy is valid till death. The survivors will be paid out in full. Dying is a pleasure.

A full moon is moving behind the black birch trees.

There aren't many who know how to go under, who can go off the rails lock stock and barrel, can clamber out with crushed hands. The majority die in clubs. Die like a rat, simply come to a stop. Are still rats, only no longer functioning ones. Death as an accident . . .

SEPTEMBER

Wednesday 1st.

I was working on the 'Grog-seller's dream'[54] when little Geyer[55] appeared in a yellow mackintosh reaching to his ankles and said Cas is coming today. He has been sitting around with his relatives, no doubt doing nothing but be considerate. An understanding nod of the head means more to him than seven heavens spangled with stars, he talks big but would settle for less. R.i.p.

I've finished the 'dream', also the 'Ballade vom Mitmenschen' and then first thing this morning 'The man at the wedding'.[56] This is a good spell, I've got my hands full and suddenly the reservoirs are brimming after the summer drought. Good times like this keep recurring, no cause for despair. Apart from that I've played billiards a bit with Orge, and seen to Mother's tombstone. But tonight I want to go to the music-hall.

I went with Brüstle and saw an eccentric clown of immense stature who shot at the lights with a little pistol, banged himself on the head, developed a large bump, sawed it off and ate it. I was enchanted: there's more wit and style in that than in the entire contemporary theatre.

Once I get my hooks on a theatre I shall hire 2 clowns. They will perform in the interval and pretend to be spectators. They will bandy opinions about the play and about the members of the audience. Make bets on the outcome. Every Saturday the theatre will have a Deuxième.[57] The hit of the week will be parodied. (Up to and including *Hamlet, Faust.*) For tragedies the scene-changes will take place with the curtain up. Clowns will stroll across the stage, giving orders: 'He's about to go under, see. Dim the lights. That staircase gives off an aura of tragedy. Bankruptcy is inevitable with caryatids like that. He'll have to catch flies. That was good, the way he put his hands in his trouser pockets. The way he said "One must be as idle as a dormouse." Excellent! It's at this point

[54] 'The grog-seller's dream'. I.e. 'Exemplary conversion of a grog-seller' in *Poems 1913–1956* p. 64. See note there (p. 531) on its derivation from Wiegler's *Figuren*. It was later set to music by Weill and included in *Happy End*.
[55] Georg Geyer was a school friend of Brecht's. Later a radiologist in Berlin.
[56] 'The man at the wedding'. Another lost poem.
[57] A Deuxième. As opposed to a Première.

that the principal scene takes place. There's going to be some real crying. The heroine's got her hanky ready. Oh, how I wish it was over...' (They say all this sadly, with absolute seriousness, they are sad fellows lit in a green light, green angels preparing the Fall...) The clowns will laugh about any hero as about a private individual. Absurd incidents, anecdotes, jokes. They'll say of David 'Why doesn't he wash more often?' And of Baal, the last period, 'He's in love with that dirty tramp'. The idea would be to bring reality back to the things on the stage. For God's sake, it's the *things* that need to be criticised – the action, words, gestures – not their execution.

As I put my verses together I have in mind the way Rodin wanted his *Burghers of Calais* to stand in the market square, on such a low plinth that the real-life burghers wouldn't be dwarfed. So the mythical burghers would be as it were standing in their midst, saying good-bye. That's the way poems should stand among people.

Thursday 2nd.
Bound in with the poems:
A page with newly coined words like 'Indian legends'.
Salons on the Mont Cenis. Carnival in the blood. Etc. (Raw material for imaginative writers.)
A blank page – for a map of the area, preferably drawn in coloured crayons.
A table of contents with a lot of titles of poems that don't occur in the book at all.
Still nagging away at *Drums in the Night*. I'm drilling rock, and the drills are breaking. It's terribly hard to make this fourth act follow grandly and simply after the first three, at the same time carrying on the external tightening-up of the third, which works pretty well, and bringing the internal transformation (in 15 minutes) forcefully home. What's more, the play's strong, healthy, un-tragic ending, which it had from the outset and for the sake of which it was written, is the only possible ending; anything else is too easy a way out, a feeble concoction, a concession to romanticism. Here is a man apparently at an emotional climax, making a complete volte-face; he tosses all passion aside, tells his followers and admirers to stuff it, then goes home to the woman for

whose sake he created the whole mortal fuss. Bed as final curtain.
To hell with ideas, to hell with duty!

Friday 3rd.

Zarek has been chucked out of 'Junges Deutschland' chez
Reinhardt: ('Young Germany',[58] an outfit full of young Germans,
that's to say not German all that long, their Germanness is young.)
Karl V[59] is a vacuous botch-up, full of 'glowing' ambition which
of course people take for passion. But that chap is far too vain to be
able to do anything worth while. You can massacre yourself, but
not by flagellation. And all that nonsense about Ideas and Ideals.
The cakewalk doesn't suit a parquet floor, and that's exactly ...
Anyway, what does it matter whether you're a chap on the first
storey or one in the basement? Damn all.

I'm beginning to feel a faint prejudice against binary divisions
(strong-weak, big-small, happy-unhappy, ideal-not ideal). It only
happens because people are unable to think of more than two
things at once. That's all that will fit into a sparrow-sized brain. But
the soundest policy is just to keep on tacking. The question of costs
has to be settled by discussion. All that's needed in order to be
happy, to work well, to be able to idle, to back oneself up, is just
one thing, intensity. To be intensely unhappy means not to believe
in the cause. To make an operation of it. Amor fati. Doing
everything with all one's body and soul. Never mind exactly what.
Small *or* great: both. Not just politics, hope for the future,
sunshine all the time. See that rain? drink it. To be present at one's
own misfortune, to devote oneself to it body and soul. The only
hours that are lost – sold below market price, forced sales,
meanminded profits – are those when you had nothing to tell
yourself about things. When you didn't bellow, didn't cry out,
didn't laugh, didn't bare your teeth, didn't screw your finger into
your temples, didn't even swim or take a catnap.

I want a gesture for all that, visible from the gallery, strong
enough to smell and be carried away by, for Act 4 of *Drums*. Where

[58] 'Young Germany'. 'Das junge Deutschland' was the general title given by
the director Max Reinhardt to the programme of Expressionist plays at his
Deutsches Theater in Berlin in 1917–18, thereafter becoming that of the theatre's
magazine.
[59] *Karl V.* Play by Otto Zarek.

a man does something, then does something else (– but does it). Stirs up a whole city, drives deluded people to attack the newspaper offices, makes poor people drunk, fills them with speeches, decks them out with weapons; then goes home. Let them go to the newspaper offices, not him. He's no longer deluded, no longer poor. The main thing is the gesture with which he goes home, removes his tunic, tears off his tie, grips his throat with his hands, breathes deeply, says 'it's all a bore' and goes off to bed with his woman.

Saturday 4th.
Early this morning I read the end of Döblin's *Wadzeks Kampf*[60] and found some ideas that strike a chord. You can't base a tragedy on his hero. Mankind shouldn't be turned into tragedy. And there are splendid things about tragedy in the book. (It actually calls for reticence.) Altogether the book is a powerful one. It leaves humanity in a reticent semi-obscurity and makes no converts. That's the way things are, is the gist of its 300 pages. I love that book.

Sometimes I have qualms: could my accursed hankering for intensity be a sign that there's a weak point somewhere in the system? (Never mind, it's not important.) If there is then it should be emphasised, health salts should be rubbed into it, or the place relieved or exercised. In cases of *tabes dorsalis*[61] (caused by youthful excesses) one sees people with a peculiar stamping gait, conspicuous people, grotesque people, people with a fatal inclination to the grotesque. They walk three times as deliberately as normal people, they stamp as if they had iron weights on the soles of their feet, they don't notice when they are down. They are not forceful. They have no high spirits. Such people also as a rule carry themselves remarkably upright, they are by no means flexible, they are characters, either-or persons, they don't insinuate themselves, don't lie down, don't tack. They push everything to extremes, their upright carriage comes from their fear of their own glassy hearts. In short, they are *poor* people.

[60] *Wadzeks Kampf mit der Dampfturbine* (Wadzek's Struggle with the Steam Turbine). Novel (pub. 1918) by Alfred Döblin, 1878–1957.

[61] *tabes dorsalis.* Locomotor ataxia, a nervous disease sometimes resulting from syphilis.

In the evening went to the *Great German Passion*[62] by the Fassnacht brothers. Wretched text, tastelessly presented. And yet certain sayings from the Bible are indestructible. They go clean through one. You sit there shaken by shudders that get under your skin and run right down your back as in love. That said, the figure of Jesus needs to be characterised by intensity and nonchalance. A man for men, for the present moment, for the place where he is, breathes, talks, suffers. The whole business is poetic, unsuited to the drama, being illogical, indeed a-logical, utterly destructive of any sense of consequentiality. It's a set of mystical visions, a good man beneath a fig tree, with his heart on his lips, a living impression, a man quite without a navel, a successful creation, aimless, whose back doesn't need any sort of stiffening (fulfilment of obligations or what have you). An invulnerable man, because he puts up no resistance. Wholly prepared to tack, pliable, cloud-like, full of starry skies, gentle showers, wisdom, cheerfulness, trustfulness, possibilities. In short, *the* good man. He cannot be represented dramatically; he doesn't resist. He never confronts anything with a face of his own – that would be an affront, a piece of self-assertion, of arrogance, an interference with other people.

Sunday 5th.
Non-stop rain, poetry has run dry once more, but I've rescued one or two of my best bits from the confusion. There's a lot still swimming around there; so what's the point of binding all that stuff up yet?

Otto had fixed something with girls for this afternoon and brought Cas along, so I saw him. Not that it was Cas so much as Neher, Rudolf Neher, a school teacher's son.

> Fat Caspar's gone and left us.
> No better man than he.
> He drew, made all our portraits
> And drank prodigiously.
> He'd fill a fat hole neatly
> Then satisfied completely
> Would sleep beneath a tree.

[62] The *Grosse Deutsche Volkspassion*, a now forgotten work, was given at the Augsburg Metropol theatre.

Fat Caspar has gone paddling
Across a pitchblack lake:
Back when he went swing-boating –
Two seats he used to take –
Now fills two spaces floating
In Hell's profoundest lake.

And now Caspar has faded
Like grass that droops away –
Just as the sun was warming
The mild sky at midday.
The wind was in his quarter
His life and times grew shorter
Like grass he drooped away.

Many the front-line trenches
Where death and he played dice.
He even drew death's portrait
And sold it for a price.
They set their guns to spray him
But found it hard to slay him
For breathing was his vice.

He climbed into broad sunshine
Up where the green leaves stop.
A lukewarm wind swooped down then
And, fluttering, ate him up.
So Caspar now has faded
And got a most degraded
Layer of dust on top.

Buschiri, I and Orge
Had things to talk about
And could not help observing
How Cas had faded out.
To show we still adore him
We shed some fat tears for him
And gave his corpse a clout.

The worms must not devour him
With reptile appetite

Once more inside a fat hole
With earth around packed tight.
The drummers did what's proper
Each mourner doffed his topper.
He's lying in the night.

I've thought of various things in connection with the tale of
Malvi,[63] who dies on Tahiti. A hard man, a good man, who has one
passion, one beloved mistress: which is – walking straight. This
leads him to end up on beggars' crutches. No: he is beaten
crooked, gently buried. He holds himself well, he holds himself
badly, is held by others, is dropped. He is not easy-going, he's not
sorry for himself. He sits down in the rain which has washed out
his brains, and studies his hands. He is full of holes and secrets,
hazardous boardings-over of precipices, terrifying floors over pits
of decay, all within himself. Everything is too complicated, he
can't resolve it, he can't resolve *himself*, things are too strong (even
if there's nothing you can do about them . . .); he dies in the midst
of everything, because these things which he has (finally)
abandoned seem to be calming down and sorting themselves out
nearby, meanwhile giving off a faint light.

No: strong and weak is not the right distinction. It all lies in
between. Burning – chilling, that's exaggerated; what's merely
irritating is in a lukewarm zone. Master and man are negro
distinctions.

Nine of us in Otto's flat spent the afternoon slowly filling up
with tea and alcohol. Then came jokes, jokes not with the mouth
but with the hands. There were four girls there, I sang, but then I
chucked the guitar aside, grabbed a girl from Otto (Hansi Haase)
and carted her into the Dadaist cabinet.[64] Otto tugged at me,
forcing me to fight like a negro, in the process she hit her head on a
chair, bumped it against a cupboard, knocked it against a wooden
partition; then on to the ottoman, where I kiss the bruises, it's dark
there, she is soft, warm, pretty, we have a wrestling match, but she
doesn't want it, people pass through, a girl says 'you've got a face

---

[63] Malvi. There are other references to this project among Brecht's notebooks
of 1920.

[64] Dadaist cabinet. 1920 was the year of the Berlin Dada exhibition, and Otto
Müller had presumably decorated a corner or closet in Dada style.

like an orangutan.' I start singing again, just a bit drunk, in a top
hat, looking foul, it's a vice den, there's been some filming, then to
salvoes from the piano I'm just beginning to scribble a monologue
for Malvi on a bit of newspaper, when Cas wrecks my last chance
by giving a crude imitation of my recent performance, seizing the
girl with his arms like an orangutan, bending her till everything
cracks, flinging her against the wall, breaking her bones, in short
training her. It doesn't come off, he just makes a mess of things,
looks like a flunkey, gloomy, worried, like a pansy, stammers
synthetically, acts the simpleton, acts the brute, gnashes his teeth
so you can hear it fifteen feet off, grinds his cheekbones, oozes
vitality but hasn't got his mind on the job. Otto is lying halfdrunk
behind the desk with a girl, working away. He has drunk well,
filmed well, looks well. The women are stupid, generally speaking
no class, a slimy fat Jew is sitting there with his arm round that
Müllegger girl whom I'd brought along but didn't address a word
to; she'd better watch out what she's letting herself in for. I'm not
her nanny. I'll be sorry for her afterwards. But there's nothing I can
do about my aversions. Otto's flat is like a junk shop.

Monday 6th.
In *David* the real motions of the play need to be linked directly to
the political events; all the psychology should be dissolved in
action – because politics is too interesting to serve as mere props.
The audience's palate must be so treated that it relishes whatever is
put before it; and this must be done by catering for all its pleasures
down to the last one. The plot has become far too clear and
rational. Hebbel was a disaster. Floods are preferable to
wastepipes. It must cover your head, you swim with it, you dive,
you get seaweed in your throat, fish in your teeth, you open your
eyes under water. Piling up images makes things fateful and
interconnected, things swirl rapidly down and turn back into
muscular sensations. A lot of things have gone rigid, their skin has
thickened, they have protective coatings; these are words. There
are piles of dead houses, so many piles of stone with holes where
lights are lit in the evening and parcels of flesh walk about beneath
roofs designed to keep out the rains of heaven and the endlessness
of the terrifying star-covered sky, sheltered from all this and the
wind too, and at night the parcels lie stiffly among sheets and

pillows, their mouths open, pumping air in and out, their eyesockets closed. All this is obliterated by the word 'houses', which squats in our brain and shields us from being attacked by the thing itself. What we have in us is only so many newspaper reports of things. We see events with the eyes of reporters who only notice whatever could interest people, could be understood. At the moment this is precisely what George is on to; i.e. the things have gone over to the offensive, they are pressing him hard, he is already up against the wall wondering if he can control his brain, hold his position. He looks out of his window at an old woman who seems to him as strange as an animal, unrelated, repulsive, worn-out, stinking. She goes flying through his brain swiftly and smoothly, unembellished, skimming along some different orbit. Or he looks at a kerbstone and thinks: it's raining on a kerbstone, how odd. Rain. Kerbstone. It's raining. What is rain, actually? How tragic that splashing business is, the whole lot has got to come down, it has no choice, it's hammering the kerbstone flat, flowing into its cracks, the stone is going to wilt like a starched collar. But perhaps the stone likes it; or is there no relationship between kerbstone and rain? Do they not know one another? Why are such things there if there's nothing one can do about them? Or again he goes up to some railings one evening – it's always the evening – iron railings. The uprights stand so straight, one after another: one, two, three, four, there's no end to them, so simple. Such calculation. Such poverty. And he shakes them, they're wet from the rain. He's got wet hands. (First the railings are wet, then his hands are wet too, and they grow cold; different hands hanging from his wrists, wet hands ...) Nothing's worse than when things get encrusted in words, become hard, hurt when you throw them, lie around dead. They need to be stung into life, skinned, enraged; one has to feed them, lure them out of their shells, whistle to them, stroke them, beat them, carry them round in a handkerchief, break them in. One has one's own underclothes, every now and then one washes them. One doesn't have one's own words, nor does one ever wash them. In the beginning was not the word. The word is at the end. It is the thing's dead body. What an extraordinary creature the human being is. .... The way he takes things into his body, goes around in wind and rain, makes little young humans out of other humans, by glueing himself to them and filling them with fluids, to the accompaniment of groans of pleasure. O God, please let my sight always cut through the crust, pierce it!

Tuesday 7th.

Bit by bit I'm getting free. I've started putting on my old clothes once more: concertina trousers, thick grey socks, torn jacket and coloured shirt. I'm no longer doing so much lying around, since the women have cleared off, and am once more walking on the kerb, making faces, not caring what impression I make, but grinning so my rotten teeth can be seen. I'll soon be able to bust the mirror. What a treat for respectable people. That's what I'm like, so cheer up! Ugly, insolent, new-born, just out of the egg. (Complete with egg-skin, shit, blood, none the less.)

Cas came in with the face of a criminal under sentence. He squatted there glumly, pressing his chest against the edge of the table and waiting to hear the worst. No doubt it was worse than he expected. I socked him clean out of his skin, made that thin skeleton on the sofa see the glittering fat Cas I painted on the wall, leading him to all the right places to view it from. Smooth swords bored through him, his skin crumpled, he grew visibly older. I hit and struck, against leather; not a drop of blood came. He'd already used up his tears to paint with, thin watercolours resulted. Things were going wrong for him because *he* had gone wrong. In the evening Lud Prestel and I went down to the Lech, which has risen, with yellow waves rolling along like fat bodies as it smacks its lips and drones out a song from its swollen mouths beneath a low sky, a starry sky from which an explosion has driven the clouds away, leaving a hole in it. We talk about how things can feel. Walking along I think that this house has views about a star, some kind of relationship with it, neither friendly nor hostile but one that is more or less green or black or something of that sort. A lot of people are only able to feel themselves by means of things and the resistance they offer; their urge for activity is really an obsession for reaching their own limits, filling their own dimensions; they jostle things along in front of them, they refute themselves so that in the foggy confusion of the ensuing debate they may just for one second become convinced of their own existence. At the same time there are others who go about like sieves: things pass through them.

Wednesday 8th.

Over me like a sword hangs my inability to write the fourth act of *Drums*. It's an age of poetry. I know what's required, but have lost the impetus. The cuts in the last scene of *Baal* (Early Morning in the Forest) are another painful affair.

Have sent Hansi Haase one of the little Insel books:[65] To remind you of certain bruises after they have faced . . .

Went to a (real) bullfight film. I liked the fellow who was called Galla- something. He had such an elegant neck and bum, and the way his sword slid into those big bodies, quivering and swishing: like fate. He was miming his own death. For that's how he really came to die: mangled by a bull. The whole country went into mourning. The king prayed at his coffin. His corpse went to its grave by special train. (Before matadors go off to the bullfight they kneel down in the bullfighters' chapel and pray God to aid them in the cutting up of His animal, the entertainment of His public.)

In the evening with Otto to the Ludwigsbau.[66] The orchestra made dumplings of Smetana's *Vltava*, an inflated work, and little Haase with her squashed-up face and generous hips got every drop of honey from it. I had handled her the wrong way. Unsystematically. Then to the Lech with Otto. A starry sky: it was turning. A cool wind blowing. Otto described me as I was on Sunday. The orphan boy, so gentle that the midges walk freely over his face, suddenly counts aloud up to five and shits in the soup tureen. This child – purer than any angel – suddenly starts using his toenails to scratch people's navels out. Breaks up a flat using a lady's head. Says 'It doesn't matter . . .'

Thursday 9th.

Frank is said to have red hair, to be impertinent, to like nonsense. Bravo!

A man with one theory is lost. He needs several of them, four, lots! He should stuff them in his pockets like newspapers, hot from the press always, you can live well surrounded by them, there are comfortable lodgings to be found between the theories. If you are to get on you need to know that there are a lot of theories; a tree

[65] Insel books. Famous, still extant series of prettily bound booklets of c. 60–70 pages, often with good illustrations.
[66] Ludwigsbau. Hall in the Augsburg city park.

too has several, but only masters one of them, for a while.

I spent morning and afternoon going round with H. Haase. She's got an imposing bottom which she wraps in silk, but is stupid, salacious and boring. She's straight out of an operetta, too giddy for me. Sexy little women of her sort undoubtedly have a sound instinct for whatever is sound, are equipped with all basic needs and don't buy pigs in pokes, wouldn't pick a pigeon-chest to weep on, never listen to cloudy talk but stick to solid muscular pleasures, with a certain inborn penchant for negroes possibly, albeit a tepid one. However, I prefer my own disease any day. What I want is to bottle them and preserve them and caress them and make do with those solid clouds, with whatever's crooked, tangled, misplaced; want to be able to beat them up, knock sense into them, love them down and joke with my thighs. Better to stuff some old virgin with a skin like a dog than poke around in everybody's pet little hole. Give me brain-damaged Bertha any day sooner than her.

Why not write an operetta? Final tableau: a man with a red tie and bell-bottomed trousers singing a lyric in mid-stage:

We never make a fuss
Though we're not proud of it
It can't apply to us
So we don't mind a bit.

And if they beat you till you bruise
You needn't be distressed
If you've got something still to lose
It'll show what you once possessed.

Thereupon a lot of people slope on to the stage and join in, lots of them, in increasing numbers, filling the entire stage, wearing red ties, and bawling out that it can't apply to them.

Friday 10th.
Sunny weather, shot through with thunderstorms. I keep going around with a hollowed thorax like a bull, but in circles, and everything is overcome by giddiness. Yellow leaves spiral down on our bald patches. Almighty farts thunder through the intestines once again just like in the Bronze Age. But creation is starting to

shed its leaves and once more we practise putting our tails between our legs against the months of decline. I've been doing no work. I've just been letting my blood flow, filling my lungs and arming for war.

It's no secret: I've failed to compose an act, I've made five attempts, over a period of two years, and never got over the first hurdle; I'm ashamed and disturbed.

Re 'Malvi': Somebody keeps beating him on the head till he stomachs ... that business of eternal damnation. His foot has gone, from the knee down, he can never swim again, never more; they can play football with his foot; when he smacks his stick against his shin the stick goes clean through, whack, nothing there. Never. Never. Never. Time is trickling away, the rain is pouring, suddenly he is over, you just don't see him all, don't feel him all on your skin, suddenly he's gone.

Things are too complicated. Nobody can make any headway, they are all interconnected, they don't come together but run off in every conceivable direction, all in motion too, and time, time trickles away. Who can clear up these misunderstandings, who can disentangle the threads?

Saturday 11th.
To Munich at midday. Cinema: *Sumurun*.[67] Well directed. A second-rate play, rather crude. But you're propelled into it. I pondered over what's to be done about Holzstadt, she can't just be thrown on the scrapheap. Met Klabund. He's not making much money (1000 a month at the most. With all his plays to date 3000 M., with *Moreau* 6000). We were going to write a farce this winter. Suddenly I thought, why not a film? And during the night I roughed it out in bed with Otto, we only had one bed for the two of us, we lay squashed together with him snoring, me working on *Pope of the Mormons*[68] and meantime battling for a bit of blanket to cover my poor feet. Went to the Oktoberfest[69] and ate there.

[67] *Sumurun.* Film by Ernst Lubitsch (1920) of a play staged by Reinhardt, with Pola Negri and Paul Wegener. Eng. title *One Arabian Night*.
[68] *Pope of the Mormons.* This project does not seem to have been pursued very far.
[69] Oktoberfest. The Munich autumn fair.

Sunday 12th.
He was an irresponsible fellow, nothing worked when he was
there, he couldn't rely on himself for an instant. There were brawls
in his apartment, mortages seemed about to fall on one's head, the
walls had been sold twice over and the worm was in them. But in a
continually prolonged process of moving out he himself sat there
cheerfully and indifferently, surrounded by crates and totally
demolished articles of furniture, made the best of his hopeless
situation and smacked his lips over the senseless destruction all
round him, cheerfully refusing to become anything ('anything'
being a means, one can only become a means) and mooching round
among his setbacks, eyeing them inquisitively. It was an *end*.

Otto dragged me to the Preysing-Palais,[70] he devoured its
elegance, wallowed voluptuously in the leather armchairs, felt his
suit, bossed the waiters about. I was out of place, undignified,
could only feel my pockets, was the dirty stain on the whole outfit.
These things don't want one to talk to them, laugh at them, turn
them upside down, smack one's lips when consuming them, they
refuse to be treated as ends, punched, ogled, hacked to pieces.
They want to be quietly and effortlessly enjoyed, with one's eyes
half-shut, they won't tolerate familiarities, they don't wish to be
applauded, they are wonderfully trained servants, wonderfully
training their masters.

I also sat in the Kindl Cellar and listened to Mr. Goldschmidt[71]
talking about the Russian economic situation, a whole lot of
abstruse stuff about associations and control systems. I didn't stay
long. What alarms me about that place is not the disorder actually
achieved there but the order actually aimed for. At present I am
very much against Bolshevism: universal military service, food
rationing, controls, conspiracies, economic favouritism. On top of
that, at best: equilibrium, transformation, compromise. I say
thanks a lot and may I have a car.

[70] Preysing-Palais. Then a first-class Munich restaurant.
[71] Dr Alfons Goldschmidt, 1879–1940, one of the founders of the IAH or
International Workers' Aid, was an economist active in promoting the Soviet
cause. At the end of the 1920s he was involved as a consultant in some of Erwin
Piscator's productions. From 1925 on he was a professor of politics in the
University of Mexico.

After a long interval I have once again seen my first drunks. Like a pilgrim to Mecca catching sight of the Caaba[72] ...

Monday 13th.
Part 3 of the *David* play, with the old man shuffling alone through the rooms talking to the elders: Saul, Jonathan, Absalom, fat bodies in pallid air, aquarium specimens all four of them. David is put on the defensive, up against the wall. He is speaking. Listen! He is speaking about a water conduit. It was hard to build. There were rocks to be drilled through. Israel had no blacksmiths. It was a clever, delicate, strong piece of work, you had to be strong all the time. David is speaking of this when he sees someone laughing. Saul is laughing. 'What are you laughing for, Saul? It wasn't easy'. Jonathan asks 'Where is it? Is it working well? Do many people get water from it?' He replies thoughtfully: 'It has fallen into disrepair. Nobody needs it now. But that doesn't matter. It wouldn't matter.' He is worried because he failed to do the right thing. Did he not realise that the right thing was to be idle, to want to change nothing, be human? Why didn't he do that? Saul of course had to be shielded. Made great gestures against David and the others; they were marvellous, David bowed before them, but they had to be paid for, by David. Saul a great man, but David has to shield him. That wasn't easy. On no account did David want to let things stay as they were, go as they went before. Didn't Saul go under despite all? – if only they had watched him! Absalom, of Saul's tribe, wanted to go under too; he was another of the same sort, big, unswerving, imperious, battering his way through brick walls; he had to be shielded. There was scarcely time to take his revolt at all seriously, it was such a crazy affair, by accident it nearly strangled them; so it had to be quickly dealt with, without dignity or elegance, crudely. And Absalom couldn't have been saved. But these two had followed their own heads, and their heads wanted to batter down the wall, the wall proved stronger, their heads smashed like eggshells. It was he, and he only, who had made the wall, had acted against himself, played politics and imagined he could do something 'just for the time being'. He was unworthy, it is only right that at the end he should prove himself worthy by

[72] The Caaba. The principal mosque at Mecca.

breaking up, by keeping his wits about him and saying 'yes' all the same. He's left with Solomon, whom he despises, his own son, 'that fellow!' Smooth and hollow, the dealer, the sage, the windbag, the diplomat, the priest. Solomon, who protects no-one, kills no-one, 'uses' everyone, twists everything, who finds it all easy, who can do it with one hand tied behind his back. Solomon, who cannot break up, the trumpet merchant, the heir, the perfect gentleman. Solomon, a hundred women's darling, God's boyfriend, Israel's throne-filler. The long and the short of it: decline and fall of the strong man.

Tonight, down by the Lech with Cas, among the stars, the fourth act[73] came to me: narrow stage, large people. At night, towards dawn: it's starting to get chilly. At the end the man goes home with the woman, strong, calm, serious. Everything up to that point was convulsion, fever, nickelodeon, romanticism. Now for seriousness, sobriety, back to the old routine. A yellow streak on the horizon. Smoky sky. It's growing chilly. The woman helps him into his jacket. Quiet descends on the newspaper offices. Isolated shouts. The wind gets up.

Thursday 14th.
Fling myself into film scripts: into *The Education of G. Parker*[74] and *Pope to the Mormons.* It's raining on the yellowing leaves, in the evening the sky clears. I was at the Aichers',[75] got given tea and a headache, read the opening scene of *David*, which he's to play. It's still unfinished, in many ways too naive. I'm glad things have got moving, but am not satisfied. The image of Bi, hovering charmingly between my walls, can't drag me away. Exams have descended on Orge. It becomes harder than ever to put up with the chaos of my papers: *Summer Symphony* an unripe fruit, uneatable. *Lucky Hans*[76] a flop, a half-rotten egg. *Drums in the Night* still on the verge of an ending, but a long way from being really finished. The short stories roughly sketched out, needing more composition.

[73] The fourth act. I.e. of *Drums in the Night.*

[74] *The Education of G. Parker.* No further trace of this project.

[75] Aichers. Rudolf Aicher and Annie Aicher-Simson, actors at Augsburg municipal theatre.

[76] *Lucky Hans. Hans im Glück* (title of the Grimms' story), a play which Brecht abandoned in 1919 after completing seven out of eight scenes. The MS survives.

Baal I now find unsatisfying, it seems less fresh and spontaneous, much too polished, refined, flattened out. Perhaps there's been a general lack of seriousness, I've been messing about, doing too much, I get fine ideas, abandon myself to whatever's interesting, playful, elegant.

Warschauer has invited me to Baden-Baden for 3–5 days, rail fare found. Otto thinks I shouldn't go. That will allow me to talk to Warschauer about the possibility of a room in Berlin for this winter, also to hear about Berlin during the summer. Besides, I can call on Hedda and see her mother. And I'll have a look at Baden-Baden, that minor cosmopolis, snoop around among the ladies' dresses, snuggle against some pliant limbs, and build up reserves against flannel. Possibly I might also learn how to get sucked up to by posh people, and make a clinical study of the distinction between air and a hotel porter. (Air is pure unsullied air. Not so a porter.) Or at worst I can get disgusted with the whole thing, throw up and come back to my hut. Warschauer will pay for everything. He needn't get up. I shall arrive by railway. He can arrange it with money, but I can manage it without money. Anyway it's nice of him, I'm grateful to him for not demanding gratitude. I'm conducting a campaign in all directions against the bourgeois conviction (even if it were to crop up with me) that money is something so precious that it might oblige one to pay for it on the personal level. One can go ahead and take money, otherwise they just keep it from you. Since it is my practice to give presents without asking anything in return, I can also accept presents without giving anything in return for them.

Recently my fingers have developed a prejudice against comparatives. They all follow this pattern: a squirrel is smaller than a tree. A bird is more musical than a tree. Each of us is the strongest man in his own skin. Characteristics should take off their hats to one another, instead of spitting in each other's faces.

Orge said: 'This is how they imagine it is. The clever live off the stupid and the stupid live off their labour.'

Otto said: 'Seven days in the week they're wiping your arse for you and holding your cock for you as you piss, then their head gets so swollen they need a shoehorn to get their hat on, and you have to slam them against the wall because scraping them off again is the only way to get them clean. They've used their braingrease to wax your boots with, and now it's all gone they take their sweaty feet and kick you in the balls.'

Cas said: 'Your *Baal* is as good as 10 litres of schnaps.'

Midday 15th.

Chinese proverb: 'When the sands run against people, people should go away.'

At lunch Papa was talking nonsense about Communism. Two apples had been stolen from our garden; I stuck up for the thief: trees' produce can't be anybody's property. At that Papa started shouting that according to the papers the Allied Commission had instituted closing time at 11 o'clock, that's what Germany has come to thanks to people like us. He'd like to know what I've done for the community so far, absolutely nothing at all. In five years' time I'll still not have my first medical degree. High time I did a proper job of work. My literary achievements in his personal view amount to nothing at all. It all has to be put to the test still. I left quickly. So far I haven't earned anything.

We are spongers, the last human beings not to be servants. Baal and Karamazov are of our company. What's a poem worth? Four shirts, a loaf of bread, half a cow? We don't make merchandise, we just make gifts.

In the afternoon I went to the movies. In the evening I mooched along the avenue, already resonant with the golden gongstrokes of Autumn. The big poplar at the edge of the water, which has its roots in the municipal lake, is still spinach-green, but the chestnut trees are already turning. Children were fishing chestnuts out of the moat. I walked between the trees in somewhat gloomy silence.

I've read two things of Döblin's: first *Wadzeks Kampf* and now *Wang-lun*.[77] It's very powerful stuff, everything is set in motion, the relations between people are established with exceptional sharpness, everything to do with mime and gesture is brilliantly assimilated into psychology, and the scientific side relegated elsewhere. Technically, what made a particularly deep impression on me was his cultivation of the verb. Verbs have long been my

---

[77] *Wang-lun.* Döblin's novel *Die drei Sprünge des Wang-lun* (1915), thought to have influenced the temple scenes in *Man equals Man*.

weak point. I've started working on them (since reading Lorimer[78] and Synge[79]). Have gained a tremendous lot from this. The danger: Döblin's baroque style.

Thursday 16th to Tuesday 21st.
Guest of Warschauer at Baden-Baden. He relieved me of luggage and worries, conducted the band, presented me 'his' Baden, made me at home in this fashionable setting and got me to absorb the scents of trees, the rustling of dresses, light music of all kinds. He was brimming with Spengler's great work[80] and sang arias to Zionism. This country we live in will soon be finished, is over, going to the bottom; and nothing is better than Zion.

He has too much sense of purpose, wraps a meaning into every situation, believes in progress and thinks that every amoeba is sooner or later bound to turn into a monkey. But he introduced me to Lao Tzu,[81] who agrees with me about so many things that he keeps on being astounded.

On one occasion Hedda was there. We rolled around under foggy trees and a gently dripping sky, smelling the damp rotting leaves; our quarrel flared up again, she wept into her hands, this winter she has to go to Berlin. Under her veil she is pallid, sickly, beautiful. Everything jars her, everything turns aside from her, her oldest friends trample on her. And I told her 'It may be the happiest time of your life, and you're not too badly off and you should be more grateful', and 'Heap anything you can on me, I've a broad backside'. And once I took her in my arms, and it began to get better, and I also kissed her and was gentle with her. The three of us had supper together, and tonight I took her to the station.

For Warschauer: Baden & Lao Tzu.

Wednesday 22nd.
Augsburg. Idleness. I kill time with matchsticks. I take a critical view of the weather. I walk till I'm exhausted.

[78] G. H. Lorimer, 1867–1937, editor of the *Saturday Evening Post*. Brecht liked his *Letters From a Self-Made Merchant to his Son* (1902).

[79] J. M. Synge the playwright, 1871–1090.

[80] Spengler's great work. Presumably *The Decline of the West*, which started appearing in 1918.

[81] Lao Tzu. Chinese philosopher (c. 570 BC), author of the book bearing his name which later also became known as the *Tao te ching*, one of the oldest Taoist classics.

Thursday 23rd to Friday 24th.
Collected Bi in Buchloe[82] and brought her to Munich. She had grown fat, instantly sensed my disappointment and became sober and heavy. A dismal night, slept a lot, deprived of poetry. I couldn't really recapture my form, felt a bit of a waif. Next morning things improved, we went out looking for places to live, our relationship is back to normal – no improvement. The old gracefulness has rather vanished.

Otto had promised to come to Munich first thing on Thursday to help find rooms for us and look at a flat for me. He didn't need to do this, but he didn't turn up either. He had gone out to Landshut[83] to see Orge, who was sitting his exam. They sailed in during the afternoon: Otto was disagreeable to Bi, and instantly dragged Orge out again, kept on haranguing him as he tottered round in his brown suit looking white as chalk, smoking cigarettes.

If it had been anyone but Otto it wouldn't particularly have mattered; one would have swallowed hard and written him off. But all Otto's got is his reliability, and he does nothing but lie around, exploiting one for his intellectual work and buying patent-leather shoes. Otto can't take it. The charge-sheet is:

1. The abduction to the Möhringen family.
2. The pogrom against Max the Newsman.
3. The Munich Capitulation.

Re. 1: He dragged me off to the Lehrers, *stuprandi causa*, made me sing to the guitar, failed to leave with me at the right time, a plain case of rape.
Re. 2: He went off with Plärrer Elise, left me waiting and made that chatterbox Max the Newsman think me a fool to have counted on him.[84].
Re. 3: He has stopped talking about this, is too cowardly to start, keeps out of my way.

Bez[85] is defunct, Cas has been stamped into the solid earth with a stone on top of him saying 'Here lies Cas'. These things cry to

[82] Buchloe. Twenty-five miles south of Augsburg.
[83] Landshut. On the Isar about forty miles north-east of Munich.
[84] Max the Newsman, the Lehrers, 'Plärrer Elise', all unidentified.
[85] Bez. Otto Andreas Bezold, Augsburg friend of Brecht's.

heaven on Otto's behalf, but it won't help him: if he must die, then die he must.

Friday 24th.

The German drama is going right downhill, it seems, rapidly, willingly, obediently. The Berlin theatre capitalists are taking over its assets, forming the whole thing into a monopoly, the film all the time is pulling the mat from under it, has been pulling might and main for months now, disaster is sitting in the galleries, in the stalls, finally in the stage box and having a look as well. Now the rats are starting to leave the ship; Reinhardt's pulling out, Kerr[86] has entrenched himself in Valhalla and reports that it's all 'so beautiful'. But we propose to take up our quarters in her and stand straddling the deck and see if we can't make her move ahead. Perhaps we'll drink up all the water that's leaked in through the hole in her side, perhaps we'll hang our last shirts from the yardarm to serve as a sail, and blow into it (that's your wind) and fart at it (there's your storm). And go to the bottom singing so that when the ship gets there she will have some content.

It's a mild night with stars above the thin foliage. They're playing skittles at the inn Zum Kreuz and trumpets in the Popular Education Centre. I however am horribly restless and fidgety. There's a devil in me, it looks as if he's about to start by getting in among the sows. I've been running around like a demented dog and am unable to do anything. Moreover a lot of things are falling apart.

Why am I too much of a coward to look major injuries in the (squinting) eye? I always realise at once what hamstrings me: the fact that I have no power over anybody. That anything I'm given is a favour. That favours can legitimately be refused. It's a fact that I am unable to achieve the last (woodcutters') scene of *Baal* even though the type has already been set. Orge wanted to help me. It went wrong earlier; so he changed his mind. Then he said he had wanted to but I hadn't. I gulped and gave him the scene once more. He was slaving away for his exam, hadn't the time. I pushed and pushed, got two notes from Georg Müller the publisher. So I

[86] Kerr. Alfred Kerr, 1867–1948, the leading Berlin theatre critic, wrote for the *Berliner Tageblatt*.

asked if we could have a session in Munich. He said 'Friday'. I arrived punctually at midday and we started. Then Otto turned up, the atmosphere became chilly, Otto talking utter rubbish. I was nauseated, I knocked him down on Orge's bed, he pushed off in dudgeon. Orge however with him. They gave me their hand, or rather Orge did: 'Grüss Gott'.[87] Orge said he'd be through by 9 or 9.30. I came about that time, there was Otto, removed himself lentissimo, making an appointment for 10 o'clock. Orge talked about *Baal*, then after half an hour walked off in mid-flight; I walked with him, not offended, couldn't grasp what was happening. At the Schmidtberg there was a short-circuit: the scene's wrong. Otto rolled up. I asked George if he'd got something important to say to Otto. 'No, just going to the café.' George pondered as we went, coughed up one or two morsels, which he tossed to me, looked persecuted, regretful, overworked. Otto kept hurrying on, ten paces in front of us, hurrying away his hope of salvation, hurrying out of the brothel, hurrying into his student fraternity; finally just walked away. And George, without resolving anything, shook hands embarrassedly and went after him, cool, liberated, a bit cowardly following a really bad action: he won't find it helps him. (Tomorrow off he goes to join Fanny ...) I'm not furious, I simply have a bitter taste in my mouth, choke it back, would like to swallow it, can't get it down, it's nothing, absolutely nothing. It's ludicrous considering it's all about literature, but I did humiliate myself, and I was powerless. I'm nothing. I feel ashamed.

Writing tragedies is a disgraceful pursuit. Despite all our efforts it's so certain that nothing else is going to happen, nothing adds up right, nothing really matters any more. Why crawl into these wretched little outer coverings, which itch and are riddled with holes? Why loaf around among these debased, sparse and arbitrary thought processes? And everything else is lies, and this is a lie too. I haven't been unlucky, my roof is intact. My new clothes are still imbued with leprosy, I have never been beaten for my many offences. But Bittersweet[88] has grown fat, dear old Cas has been a stinker, faithful Heigei has done some successful business deals,

[87] 'Grüss Gott'. 'God greet you'. Common form of greeting in Bavaria and Austria.
[88] Bittersweet. Bi Banholzer.

then less successful ones, then about turn; and Orge, our poor brother That's All,[89] went off to the café with his patron. The ghost our nannies used to frighten us with has manifested itself; it was wearing a bed-jacket.

Saturday 25th.
Towards morning I had a dream. Someone showed me a bare room and said 'There were artists sitting there. To start with they got several cords of wood, and as soon as these were used up they got many square metres of canvas, and when this had been transformed they got one sheet of paper.' And in my dream this struck me as sensible, and I believed that artists could improve.

In the Rhineland the negroes are sucking the soil dry. They inseminate the women by squads, get off scot free, laugh when the civil population objects. The behaviour of the German civil population has been exemplary; there have been no reports of murder or manslaughter. These people whose wives have been ruined are miles away from anything resembling lynch law. They gnash their teeth, they go and do it in the lavatory so nobody can hear. They don't nail those negroes[90] to the door, they don't saw them in two, they clench their fists in a sack and masturbate in the process. They are proving that they are getting their deserts. They are what's left over from the great war, the scum of the population, cut-down loudmouths, dehumanised cattle in the mass, German citizens anno 1920.

I'm continually worried about the slight degree of power man has over his fellows. There is no universally understood language. There's no gun that hits the target. Influences operate in quite a different way: they rape people (hypnosis). This thought has plagued me for several months. It mustn't be let in, as I can't move out.

I'm very much on my own, playing billiards in the attic, reading R. Tagore's *The Home and the World*,[91] not eating much, thinking in

[89] That's All. Brecht uses the English phrase here and elsewhere as a nickname for Georg Pfanzelt.

[90] negroes. Refers to French colonial units, part of the allied force occupying the Rhineland.

[91] Tagore. Rabindranath Tagore, Bengali poet, novelist and dramatist, 1861–1941.

visual images and showing myself a film version of my rise to fame. But on the whole I am going to ruin because with comparatives exploding on all sides things are getting hostile towards themselves and me.

Sunday 26th.
It's damned exhausting continually trying to figure out new ways to stretch and extend oneself. Autumn is gaining ground from day to day, I love that. Am incidentally reading Tagore's *The Home and the World*, a wonderful book, strong and gentle.

ABOUT THIS SUMMER:

I haven't done much; swam a bit, read a thing or two, loved nothing. It was not a time of poverty, though. I had to dig around and accustom myself to the sight of corpses. Worse than the lack of achievement was the fact that a lot was started. Oh well, one or two ballads got finished. I'm getting on with sawing away the branch I'm sitting on, if only slowly. But I shall manage to lose my sense of security all right.

February to May 1921
'While the grass is growing the horse will die'
Bert Brecht.

FEBRUARY

Wednesday 9th.
It's Ash Wednesday, the day when one's so awake and pure and
mends one's ways. Napoleon's death mask reposing on the
washstand, snow on the ground outside, in the bed a bloodstain.
We went to Steinicke's;[1] Cas, Otto and the Feuchtwangers were
there too. I danced with the woman, but then I ran away and
danced cheek to cheek with **Marianne**. Soon after we got in a car,
full of bergamot liqueur, and whizzed home. Also hanging around
there were the unfortunate Mrs. Jörgen,[2] wearing white make-up,
sick (what's more, she made up to me, but I took Mar's hand) and
little Edith Blass, who's getting so old she'll be losing her teeth any
day now. I couldn't go to sleep: Mar said I'd been dancing in a
sensual way with **Mrs. Feuchtwanger** and all the women were so
insignificant. At one point she felt sick, at another she cried
because she hasn't had a child, and then she looked marvellous,
much should be forgiven her. At the ball she was dressed as a page
and was the most beautiful woman there and handled the men
marvellously, all pure and regal and quiet and cheerful and
unapproachable yet not proud. She was the only one with any right
to go to the ball, because she didn't fit there. It was organised solely
for her, but that meant nothing to her.

Sunday 13th.
Augsburg. Afternoon with the Aichers. I got **Recht** to act.
Richard III. He exhausted all his villainous gestures in no time. I
also saw the limits of his temperament. At one point he refused to
pick up a knife (I had one too): he's a coward. In bed Mar told
some shabby little stories. On one occasion matters weren't going
well, and he started stealing. He stole things wherever he went. At
her parents', her brother's etc. He actually broke into her parents'
cupboard. Now he has been in trouble again somewhere. There
was some firm for which he had the right to sign, and he stole
money from it, some of it straight out of the till, and now on being
threatened with exposure he has threatened to expose the firm for

---

[1] Steinicke's. Art gallery in the Schwabing district of Munich.
[2] Mrs Jörgen. Not identified.

its shady dealings. All this he has been doing for the very woman who says he makes her sick. Now she has been to her brother's, but he had said nothing to R. She told him herself: she doesn't want to get married till the summer and he must sleep somewhere else and it would do him no good to make scenes. At that he became small and timid, promised whatever she asked and ran away and wept. And he loves Macchiavelli. Then after all she let him sleep with her that night, he didn't touch her, and she didn't want to give it to him all at once, he was rather touching.

Monday 14th.
We spend the whole night together. She has changed. Now there's something childlike about her, something uncertain, small gestures and at moments a breathless little voice. Once I couldn't take her, had to leave her, then she laughed, quite softly and happily, and mocked me. 'That's just what's needed, a good thing that you can't always make it, my stock is going down. That's excellent.'

Tuesday 15th.
Have been slogging away religiously at the *Pirates*[3] with Cas. He is all for Marianne. What we've done is quite intimate. There's a lot of Bi in it. Life of a woman. Grows up on the savannahs and is lugged across every conceivable ocean.

Thursday 17th.
Georg Kaiser's case.[4] He committed childish thefts because his wife and children were hungry. Now he has been making pretentious speeches and parading like a peacock in the full splendour of his writerdom. Puts forward his entire work as a nervous disease. His wife is marvellous, anxious but calm, treating him like a child. The court amazingly understanding and courteous.

[3] *Pirates.* A film scheme of which no trace remains.
[4] Georg Kaiser. The dramatist, 1878–1945, author of *From Morn to Midnight* (see p. 113). He was being sued in Munich for selling articles from a house that a patron had lent him.

Friday 18th and Saturday 19th.
6 p.m. to 9 a.m. Marianne at Kraal 3.[5] Then Siebentischwald.[6]
Coffee.

Sunday 20th.
P.m. Recht, the Aichers, Ma in the Park house. Last night at the
Aichers' Ma started being so cheeky, picking up my cigarette and
smoking it, offering me bits of ham on her fork etc. Today we are
playing 'come and get me'; I put the brake on. 10–10 at Kraal 3.

Friday 25th.
Film plans looming up. New theory of money: comfortable,
elegantly cut, broad grey trousers, well hitched up; soft squashy
hat, out-thrust face, rather sharp; relaxed to the point of
recklessness – but respecting the tangible, which is merely work
rendered visible; continually weeding out, resuming, duplicating;
all for friends, for every sort of undertaking. But on the side;
raking up the solid gold. Even where the ground has been
softened. Washing gold. Piling it up, investing it, letting it
circulate, always overlooking the means (this being gold) and
looking to people, who have to work, loaf, be free to do silly
things. No ambition: what the fellow can do, he should. It's not
my job to provide the best sausage.
   Often my mind turns to Marianne, who goes by car any time she
likes. Is prepared to be given fur coats, rings, dresses. For herself.
Should one rescue her? I can't pay for her or her things. And what
am I? An impertinent little packet, you can't see my face yet, a
certified promise, and what does that bring in? Clothes, soap, a
well-lit flat, theatre, good food, music, higher feelings, laziness,
other people's esteem, lack of friction, travels, beauty, youth,
health, art, freedom? All that to be chucked down the drain for the
sake of a physiological impulse which disappears as soon as it is
satisfied! Or is it that I seem all right because I'm always changing?
That with me one can have good lighting, theatre, enjoy one's food
better, feel music, feel strong, be free to work for something, enjoy

---

[5] Kraal 3. Brecht's term for the attic room where he lived in his father's
Augsburg house.
[6] Siebentischwald. Park in Augsburg's southern outskirts.

esteem, enjoy adventures, do without travels; and on top of that
have strength, freshness, novelty, confidence? None of which is
certain . . .

And I can't get married. I must have elbowroom, be able to spit
as I want, to sleep alone, be unscrupulous.

7 p.m. to 9 a.m. Marianne at the Kraal. I read her the Wake scene
from '*Sommersinfonie*' and she thought she could play it. Me too.
But last night in bed I had an idea: the play ought to end like this:
the woman gives in, and sticks with Tauli, the bad man. I.e., she
gets over her collapse, she masters her weakness by being
dogmatic, she derives all possible strength from her resolution.

Saturday 26th.

One can see where the danger lies: whatever's left over,
underdeveloped, undigested, the remnant that one no longer
controls. Gradually we clog up with unresolved affairs, half-
masticated events. We get poisoned by the unexpended portion.
Whatever's been buried sleeps badly. Instead of helping us digest
it, the earth spews it out. What the wind failed to dry and the rain to
wash away is now growing, and this is poisoning the earth.
Corpses are the product of fear. The fear lives on. Why can't the
Jews be got out of the way? Because they've been quartered,
broken on the wheel, tortured and spat at for the last thousand
years. But the spittle gives out before the Jew does. How sad, how
devastatingly bitter are those powerful events which we try to
resist, liars that we are, by the invention of Tragedy. Every time
Reason's mouth has been blocked with earth the stifled outcry has
left a gap across the centuries. The cup was refused, and the
tragedy never took place (and became necessary).

Sunday 27th.

Clear, sunny days, I'm getting back on form. Still full of bugs, but
more resistant. The pogrom is approaching. Everything in order,
but at what a cost! Marianne's no longer thinking of marrying
Recht, she's going to marry me now; God will look this way again,
and Asia[7] will remain untouched. But as soon as I withdraw into
my shell (and icy air emanates) she faints and has blue hands, can't

---

[7] Asia. The allusion is unclear.

get at me any longer. She said something that jarred chez the Aichers, after I'd been squirming for hours, I said I wanted to go, we walked home in silence (to her place), patched it up, prudently separated, as it was late and she has a rehearsal tomorrow; and then she sits up there, and hurries to the balcony to see if I haven't come back to play Romeo, whistling in the gutter. After writing a letter to say there was something wrong with her, she was fainting too easily, she rang up next day at lunchtime.

Monday 28th.
There is such a lot cooking. Otto every now and then shows the corruptness of his attitude to money, he depends on it more than any of us. Orge was short, I gave him 300 from my savings account, all he kept was the 200 which I owed him, and Otto, without asking, helped himself to the other 100. (50 more than he was due or needs, and despite the fact that he spends his time complaining about me to Orge. But that's a form of camouflage ...) And Orge's got nothing, and I owe 120 to Klette,[8] whom I don't know. Anyway my budget never balances. But Otto, who's unable to get a woman himself (I've spoken to la Reutter and la Günzburger[9] about him) launches a great attack on Marianne, in swinishly crude terms. With the result that Orge refuses to collaborate on the film I'm supposed to be doing for Stuart Webbs[10] because I want Marianne to have a part in it (quite by the way). Orge, the old pedagogue, thinks I've got too many women and feels he's exploited every time one borrows a pin from him. And is jealous of Cas and Otto, in a permanent huff. And the corruption of all those children is to be laid at my door. I'm the politician, the mercenary brute, the shop steward, the reformer. And he is the saint of the dog coppers, the sage of the Klaucke district,[11] the great ascetic. He was telling me himself that he couldn't have Fanny (with me the expression he uses is 'couldn't

---

[8] Klette. Dr Werner Klette, Munich film critic who acted as agent for Brecht's film stories.

[9] Reutter and Günzburger. Unidentified women.

[10] Stuart Webbs. Munich company making film serials featuring a detective of that name. Started by the producer Joe May, with Ernst Reicher as director and principal actor.

[11] Klaucke district. Part of Augsburg lived in by Pfanzelt and the Brechts.

give the emperor his bath') once because she had the curse and once because he couldn't make it, and now he has been proclaiming the dogma of the Untouched Orange (improves if you look at it, and thereby remains unchanged). He is vindictive, though he says he isn't. He wouldn't draw B.T.'s fangs, when it could have been done at a price. That's when he let her piss on him. But later when he was sitting in Asia and she had no protector he had to work out a diabolical plan for her extermination. (So that Meyer & Co. should not get pissed on). He told me 'You wanted to beat them up once, and I couldn't do it. The blows would have been passed on to Fanny. Then when Fanny had gone away I wanted to do it and you didn't. Why? Because there were some books you wanted to borrow from B.T.' He can't get the idea. And Otto, who should know all about it, does nothing to dissuade him. He needs that. So the whole villa is starting to stink, and there isn't any wind.

MARCH

Tuesday 1st.
The Webbs film is still-born (15 000 Marks), but Ma was here from
8–8 and it's very good. Springtime in the Kraal.

Cas was waiting in Munich, my Cerberus. We wrestled with
Stuart Webbs. I'm horribly tired. Cas is thick as a plank.

Ever since *Galgei* I've been almost unbeatable at plotting. But
this mechanical stuff ... Then I invented something: a rotating
brothel with a respectable front. If only it were possible to rake up
some gold. If this one comes off, then another 2–3 films for Webbs.
(Start of the film à la Raffles). Those three pirate films for
Marianne, then finish. In the spring, *Galgei*. A few ballads of the old
sort, like the Orge songs.

Wednesday 2nd.
In the morning Cas and I worked on the Webbs film *The Rotating
Wine Bar*.[12] Cas acted as midwife and took over the groaning too.
He gets the pains, I get the child. At midday Marianne arrived. We
went to the zoo, where I was deeply impressed by sun, monkeys,
pinetrees, and emus (black birds with a thin neck, a fat belly, huge
sensitive eyes and a blood-red throat with a red cord tying the two
bits of the beak together). Spent the night sleeping.

Thursday 3rd.
In the early morning to Mar with a verse in my head:

> Yes, that was poor old Marianne
> Whose fate could make you weep
> She never had America
> To sing her off to sleep.

and

> When she was worried now and then
> 'In my young days', she'd say
> 'Father was always in some dockside den
> And mother miles away.'

[12] *The Rotating Wine Bar*. Became the film story *The Mystery of the Jamaica Bar*,
included in Brecht's *Texte für Filme I*, published in 1969.

Then I bundled M. into the train, went to Cas's, spent an hour listening to Kehrer's course on Cézanne, ate in the students' refectory, dictated 'The Secret of the Wine Bar' to Klette for Stuart Webbs; I'm delighted with it. And in the evening called on little Zarek, who's ill: male midwife to the Kammerspiele,[13] boyfriend to that rubber-merchant (Neuhofer[14]), who uses a french letter to masturbate. I took David along, as he's quite 'nice' and I'm fond of flowers, of whatever sort. What a script, so white-hot it's half charred, it's still wriggling around, rolling, rearing up, putting up a pretence of life ... As I hit the sack the ceiling is filming The Mystery of the Jamaica Bar.

Saturday 5th.
Spring weather. I've been reading (only at mealtimes) Döblin's *Wallenstein*.[15] What a pity that it should show off its muscles so, be so full of hysteria,. so packed with externalities dressed up in supercolossal style. What baroque! What a (politically neutral) panorama! What a risky affair (ideologically speaking): this seemingly democratic way of portraying things! The whole thing so fat, gobbets of colour and all so overemphasised, tarted up like a newspaper serial and seen strictly from the outside. *Wadzek* is incomparably more effective. In *Wadzek* the style acted as a magnifying glass, you couldn't see without it. In *Wallenstein* it is window glass, and you see things wrong. (Because nothing is ever what it looks like – through a window.)

Pay no attention to people's deeds, don't go by their opinions. Both can be misleading. What happens to people is beyond all belief. Why should I bother about people's mistakes? Am I to go into the differences between Tom, Dick and Harry? Ruin my eyesight? A woman allows a man to strangle her, sell her as bed-fodder, swear at her, lets her parents be abused and stolen from, lets the man swindle, break safes, go on his knees and beg for money from the employers he has cheated; and sleeps with him without being in love with him. She lets herself be taken by the chap the man passed her on to, years later, even though it nearly

---

[13] Kammerspiele. The most enterprising of Munich's state theatres, directed by Otto Falckenberg, where Zarek was dramaturg.

[14] Neuhofer. Not identified.

[15] Döblin's *Wallenstein*. Appeared in 1920.

killed her, so she says, she has an abortion, she messes around, she allows the rapist 'at least' to work on his own account, she allows herself, already in love, to be dragged round by filthy impertinent young fellows who kiss her and treat her familiarly, she is nice to the man because he's going away, she sleeps with a vile young fellow who plays the page and kowtows to the man he is deceiving, whose qualities he recognises; already in love, she lets him give her perfume; he says everything he possesses smells of it. And yet, even though all this is true and no-one knows what else she is going to get up to, she is a good woman, childlike and dependable and in no way to be compared with others.

In the evening Mar and Recht were at the theatre: I went out and met Recht at 'Maxim'.[16] Then he left and went to the 'Lamm',[17] asking me to send M. over. When she arrived he was hunching himself into his overcoat. She sat down with Cas and me, he came up: 'You coming? I can't hang about with my coat on.' But she stayed seated. 'I'll come on later.' Exit in a fury. After a bit I asked her to follow him and she said, smiling, but with underlying bitterness, 'Now you're sending me away.' We left together. (I'd suggested we say goodbye before leaving so she could go ahead: she refused.) She then took us along with her to the 'Lamm', but I didn't want to. (Kept making boobs ...) Subsequently Cas and I followed them and I hung round her house. No light in her window. They must have gone for a long walk. And since she stopped sleeping with him he has carried a swordstick.

Sunday 6th.
Cas and I talked about various things. He can't work from nature. Not good enough for him, he says. He still has Flanders. But his old stock is swamping his pictures. He's got to start from scratch. Paint faces like still-lifes, landscapes like faces; not paint the outside of a container but its hollow space. He's always painting things that have gone romantic.

Monday 7th.
Having drunk schnaps I sat under the red lantern and wrote in my

---

[16] 'Maxim'. The Maximilian Restaurant in the Augsburg street of that name.
[17] Hotel Weisses Lamm, close to the Augsburg municipal theatre.

shirtsleeves. Even though it's cold; but you only live once. It's only when you're drunk that you are responsible for your actions. Perhaps one day I'll do *Galgei* and have people piss schnaps into his brain and make him a public convenience like all the rest.

I wrote guitar accompaniments to 'Franziskas Abendlied' and 'Der Taler' for Marianne.[18] That was fun, and perhaps it will be some help to her.

Tuesday 8th.

In the morning I wrote the 'Ballad of the Love-sick Pig'[19] for Recht. To Munich at midday, dictated first act of *Mystery of the Jamaica Bar* to Klette. He squatted there with his mouth agape, finished up with a headache, having done nothing. Pancakes, Bi, station. Standing by the train are Recht and Marianne. Taken by surprise, I went up to them, got in, then heard words being bandied: 'Who do you think you are? Is that a way to treat me? I'll slap your face right and left for you. You stay there.' She got in, he tugged her back, she asked would I help her, I helped, saying 'Stop that. You'd better come along.' He came. She felt sick. Said 'Don't leave me today.' Then he sat beside her with a sinister grin, patting his swordstick. She raised a smile. I smoked, did my best to restore calm. Suggested she go to the Aichers'. We drove there by car. He asked me to keep out. I looked at Marianne and came along too. He was seething. 'So far I've kept my temper. You're not to come along. I won't be responsible for the consequences.' Silent journey. She looked as if she'd been raped. Then Aicher, white as a sheet, eyes popping, trembling, at a loss for words. Recht: 'You go home, don't push me too far. If you want to act as this lady's knight errant you'll have to take the consequences.' 'I am taking them. What do you intend to do about it?' Aicher: 'Just go. What am I supposed to do? Just go away.' Recht: 'Come out to the hall.' He shut the door in my face. I pushed him out of the way, fairly sharply. 'Stop that! You're crazy.' I stood in the entrance laughing. Aicher kept begging me to go. Recht shouted agitatedly: 'Keep your nose out of my affairs!' Marianne said, trembling: 'You go

---

[18] The songs are from Wedekind's *Lautenlieder*, published in 1920.

[19] 'Ballad of the Love-Sick Pig'. 'Historie vom verliebten Schwein Malchus': not one of Brecht's best poems. German and English texts in *Manual of Piety*.

home, I'd like to sleep here, Rudi.' Then on his agreeing: 'You innocent young man.' (She was still play-acting.) I walked off. When I went by later all the staircase windows were lit.

Wednesday 9th.
Thinking it over calmly I think she ought to go away now. Accept no more money, refuse to admit him, if the worst comes to the worst call the police. If he shoots he shoots. Aicher's a broken reed. I can do little or nothing, not having any money. She can survive for some months, though she's got enough money, jewels etc. for that – then go to Austria with her parents. In case of real difficulty to Hedda's in Berlin.

We met at midday and drove to the Siebentischwald. I told her she was handling Recht all wrong, taking him seriously. And still accepting money. R. doesn't run his head against a brick wall, only against rubber ones. When all's said and done she wants to mollify him, and he knows it. His last recourse isn't to his swordstick but to blubbering. Yesterday he started strangling her. He's threatened to murder her again and again. She needs to get hold of a weapon, she is entirely defenceless. If he attacks her she must shoot him down like a mad dog. It's better to go away, perhaps, but he's bound to follow her.

4–7 Kraal. That was fine. When she's happy she is very sweet and young. When there are scenes she gets old and looks as if she were past it. She's got so much to hide, and it's an effort. Her colleagues call out 'Grüss Gott, Mariandel!' Then she tells me she'd asked them what they were on about, and they'd told her that was what they proposed to say every time if I was there. The secretary behaved badly, so she made a scene outside his box and insisted that he must apologise or else Recht would sock him one. The ways of the theatre. That isn't the reason why I don't want to marry her, though. It's because I simply cannot; have to be free, have to sleep. And am nasty, a periodic monster. And they cut your nails and comb your hair and feed you to death and try to see into your sleep and go into the woods with you. They put onions to their eyes when you want to be free,   poison themselves with bitternesses as with morphine, and serve up their corpse for your tea. You are the actor with his soup plate, there'll be no applause till you lick your plate clean and sing the cook's praises. Your pissing is forgiven, because you are a pig. And the most ghastly thing of all: you only see the worst aspects of your partner, because you are yourself embittered and have tears in your eyes and your partner is embittered too.

Thursday 10th.

We may be like quiet guests and drowned fishes but there's all sorts of restlessness around us, and the beasts creep under the tables snarling. The rooms can be scrubbed white and the beds clean, but people have died of plague in those beds and the rooms have been empty a long while. Even though we say nothing, so they imagine, we've got too much to keep silent about, and everybody's frightened of our secrets. Over the fields come mice, at the same (spring)time as ourselves; and we have eaten up the last crusts. Nobody knows quite why, but we are not liked. We smell of quicklime...

I might write scene 3 of *Galgei*. In which they hire someone and it's done with papers: such is the spirit of our time. When things get so murky and involved, then you have to have recourse to papers; and that's security for you. Papers are something secure, writing is better than action, there's a space between writing and action; paper duplicates, simplifies. You see what is not there, has numbers, what is innumerable: you can choose between different numbers, they have no passions, no heads of their own. Watch, he puts his signature to a paper, and there stands Pick, that's him, the paper applies only to Pick.[20] Now he is Pick, though he still has Galgei's clothes on,

I think if the two of them are parted there'll be bloodshed after all. On the one hand this cardboard spewer of monkey's blood, this poor man's Napoleon with his swordstick and self-mutilation. On the other the woman, the fetish, who sanctifies his frauds, forgives his murders, lets her mother be abused, sleeps with him, lies to him out of fear, lets herself be strangled, called a whore and kept. He steals, burgles, she asks him for a fur coat even when she's sleeping with me. And at the same time she's childlike enough to want to start a child herself, to weep when it doesn't appear, to kiss me

---

[20] Pick. The butter dealer in *Galgei*. Galgei poses as him.

when I look puzzled, to cling to me with a touching impulsiveness. Meanwhile I just trot indifferently along, with an unruffled expression, appreciative and irresponsible in bed, deceitful maybe, capable of transcending my own situation, pretty cold, wholly unpolitical.

At night:

To begin with, everything is straightforward, naive, healthy. A twenty-year old grasping the cosmos. He is as he ought to be. He has a natural gift of the gab and uses it for strong, simple things. The faintly hymn-like quality of his diction he offsets by bursts of crude cynicism. Oh, the assurance of the unconquered, beginner's courage! Suddenly mistakes occur, based on wholly correct calculations. Things as they are alter their aspect or become unattainable. Oh, the indifference of the once conquered! All right, we must look at that tree politically, there's a man, let's get moving! Everyone knows a tree is a lump of wood. But one gets tired. It isn't much of a game. Lying is fine if one can think of something. But then he starts becoming aware of the meaning of relationships, secrets disclose themselves. What a lot happens to the tree, how hidden all that is, how it manages to control its face so it always looks the same! The formulae don't tally, they were short-cuts, sand in your eyes. His power isn't exhausted, but from now on it embeds itself in the works, creeps into the contradictions, goes against the wind; the speed drops, the wind has to be allowed for. The organism organises resistance to itself. This is the mirror image of decline, a hair's breadth away from total collapse. There's a galloping reduction of the chances of synthesis, diseases fall on his weakened body, confusing the position. Need for repose, formal cunning, a last remnant of high spirits introducing a risk of extremely subtle devastation into his incredibly high-strung complexities. Again and again the intellect undermines the position. Tempered in a hundred battles, a grinning relic, lover of still-being-around, he develops a taste for smiting, stabbing, slashing, parrying; fights on any old field, becomes a virtuoso, forgets the Holy Land. At twenty-three he's already battling desperately against vanity. Gritting his teeth, he manages to do without the respect normally due to profitability. Angrily he puts up with the imprecision of his formulations, thanks to the tremendous increase in the range of material needing

to be dealt with; renounces the pithiness he admires in favour of
the truth. What he wants is just the torso.

David.

As he waits on the wall, a fat parcel of flesh, hairy, perspiring,
lonely; as he waits, as the hours pass, as the insurrection spreads
through the country all round, he once again starts thinking in
numbers, in things and necessities, like he has done for a long
while. The peasants needed grain seed and cattle, the marriage laws
needed improving. In the south the hungry were a burden to the
farms, in the north there were no roads down which to bring the
timber. They had to be moved up there, women, children and all.
Now and again the tormented man blinked, above the tops of the
green trees, gave a quick thought to the insurrection gathering
somewhere in the south which would mean lost time and wasted
lives; then sponged it away. The aqueduct was progressing too
slowly, the treaties with the Phoenicians were due to run out. (The
insurrection was spreading through the country ...) Too many
idiots everywhere, secret acts of resistance, hostile kidnappings,
sabotage, flaws in the system. No hope of a bit of calm. (The
insurrection was spreading ...) Realities were fine. They were
consoling, despite all. You could get a footing there. People had
too many faces and too few, they had two kinds of head, two kinds
of feet, they couldn't be relied on. Started senseless insurrections,
which wasted time and material. Aqueducts decayed, fell into
disrepair or didn't work, but they were visible, distinguishable,
able to be repaired. Got water into troughs, never complained,
never even drank themselves. Knew that that was the best possible
thing: getting water into troughs. (The insurrection ...).

Friday 11th.

Last night she waited while I was asleep. She thought she could put
R. off her. But she's going quite the wrong way about it. And then
she's missed her period. A child at this point would not be so
lovely. And yet I'm pleased at the idea, utter idiot that I am.

Orge's position is becoming securer, and he is stocking up
experiences. My own experiences, having been chucked out of
doors as a result of continual changes of house, are going rotten
and getting pilfered. He has developed a kind of system. He'll soon
have restored a hierarchy. My role in his great metaphysical theatre

1a. Brecht in 1920.

1b. The Brecht family home at 2 Bleichstrasse, Augsburg, photographed in 1910. In the right-hand window are the twelve-year-old Brecht (right) and his brother Walter.

2a. Bi Banholzer and Brecht (1918/19).

2b. After the christening of Brecht's and Bi Banholzer's son Frank (2 August 1919). From left to right: Bi Banholzer, Otto Müllereisert, Caspar Neher, an unidentified woman, George Pfanzelt, Brecht and Bi's brother-in-law.

3a. Georg Pfanzelt in 1918.

3b. Caspar Neher in 1920.

3c. Gabler's Taverne in Augsburg, frequented by Brecht and his friends.

4a. Brecht in Augsburg (1920/21).

4b. A side-show at the Plärrer, the twice-yearly Augsburg fair.

5a. Bi Banholzer in 1920.

5b. Bi Banholzer in autumn 1919.

6a. One of Caspar Neher's sketches for Brecht's *Baal* (1919).

6b. Sketches by Caspar Neher for a portrait of Brecht (1919).

6c. The Municipal Theatre (Stadttheater) in Augsburg.

7a. In the Lunapark in Berlin (1923). Standing, left to right: Brecht, Frank Warschauer, Lion Feuchtwanger and his brother-in-law. Seated: Feuchtwanger's sister Franziska, Marianne Zoff, Marta Feuchtwanger.

7b. Marianne Zoff and Brecht in Starnberg in May 1923.

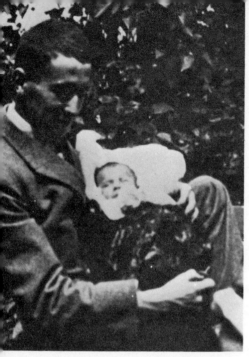

8a. Brecht with his daughter Hanne (later the actress, Hanne Hiob) in 1923.

8b. Marianne Zoff with her daughter Hanne in November 1923.

8c. Brecht in Berlin at the end of 1922.

is always that of the villain. I am the politician, the conspirator, I ruin young men and devour young women. Whatever I do he looks out for politics and finds it there. I'm supposed to pursue politics by instinct, piss out of calculation, wash in order to impress people, entertain myself in order to gain an advantage. He's got Fanny, a piece of bad taste, a dinky bit of bric-a-brac in which he invests the goodness he has been storing up. He hasn't got her entirely, here too something's wrong, there are flaws, there's something to be swept under the carpet. He suspects people don't take her seriously; people suspect she doesn't take him seriously. He scents objections, comparisons, the good old system of class distinctions. The fact is, though, that she is ruining him. As for local administration, Orge is reconciled to it, any job is equally good, it's just me who's lazy. (Forget the idea that work's no good. Because all work is equally good.) As for her virginity. Fine. One has what one fails to take. He feels propelled in a certain direction, that's nature, but he feels that I'm doing some of the propelling. I'm the glutton, the crude thinker, the vandal. There'll no longer be any grass growing behind me, so he hears. So our ways have separated. Marianne spent the night here. It's a miracle, but her period hasn't come. That chokes one's throat, something chokes in one's throat. I'd forgotten that, my God; and now God has gone and put his foot in it again. Me, I laugh and I'm good to her. She laughs too.

Saturday 12th
This morning my head was pretty full, but at noon I roused myself and saw – the sea. Come what may, it's always there at the end – the sea! Things may go badly for me, but – on my own! Her body is better than any other, she's strong and childlike, a good mother, she won't crack up easily, she has stood Recht for four years and has been raped, nearly killed by an abortion, frequently strangled, often loved and again and again been rescued. She's not yet thirty, she is beautiful and clever, she's complaisant. She should have left Recht right away, she needs a child. It'll be an ugly thing if I leave her, but what am I doing being with her, I don't earn any money and am no good, and want to wear my shirt on my body and don't care for contracts.

Tonight she came down, R. had brought her home, walked past

me swaying, blind, as if he were drunk (now he could smell me). I
didn't let her go home, where he can get in, but took her into the
Kraal, lit a fire, made up a bed on the sofa. She's in the bed, asleep.

Sunday 13th.
Now I'm getting a child by black-haired Marianne Zoff of the
brown skin who sings in opera. I kneel on the ground, weep, beat
my breast, cross myself a lot of times. The spring wind runs
through me as through a paper stomach, I incline myself. A son is
going to be born to me. Again.

Kramer[21] and I lay on the grass by the Bismarck Tower. The
grass was still yellow. Birds flew noisily over us. Kra. said 'Either a
mother or a whore.' It wasn't I who said it. The stars at night!

Monday 14th.
Rake up some gold! Munich. I dictated to Klette. He gobbled it up
like a hen, gulped, goggled, passed out (with eating). In the
evening Bi was at Otto's. We did election speeches in dumb show.
She clapped like a child. (Bi is suffering from some vaginal
infection . . .)

Hedda has sent 300 marks for me to go to Berlin with. But what
I most long for at present is to learn what I'm to do with Marianne.
She is a woman. I've got a woman in Berlin.

Tuesday 15th.
Bicycled to Starnberg with Otto. Blue, green, warm. Boating. Back
in the evening to dig for gold. Left to myself I hit the sack.

Wednesday 16th.
Spent four hours dictating to Klette. *The Mystery* is making
headway. If I can lay my hands on 5000 I'll be over the worst.
Climbed, laughing, to ethereal heights. Plunged into work; I can
feel the day *after* tomorrow; I'm killing my chicken.

Still a most beautiful heavenly blue. Sweet berries droop into
one's mouth. But that pregnant woman and that man with the
swordstick. Hush: I'm killing my chicken.

In the sun behind the infantry barracks. No period. She was

---

[21] Kramer. Not identified.

wearing a pretty knitted jacket. Such a lovely day yesterday. She'd spent money like water. This put me in a black mood: 'I'm sorry, but I haven't got money to chuck around, I'm sorry that you should be spending somebody else's. If you have to accept it in order to eat, for better or worse, there may be no alternative. But to buy blouses . . . and with my child? I haven't any money. You must control yourself. I can't do it. We're poor.' Close to one another, hard in the bright sunshine: films or nothing. 100 000 or 0. Beautiful woman, healthy child, summer, activity. Or poverty in triplicate, sweat, dirt. The days are passing, the child growing.

In the evening she sang Dorabella in *Così fan tutte*. She acts very beautifully, with calmness and grace, and sings with a slight warble, like a lark. I went quietly home.

Thursday 17th.
She said if she gives up her jewels her parents will be able to buy a farm. She will be able to live there, but only so long as we are married. Otherwise it will just be on sufferance, and she finds that impossible. So we'd have to get married. But *I* find that impossible. She stayed the night.

Friday 18th.
The Hannah Cash film.[22] In the final section the crew are drunk, tucked in the belly of the sailing ship; and she runs up the steps, evening is drawing in, there's no-one on deck and the sea is grey with rain coming down, you can't see far. She goes to the bridge where a long succession of men have stood: the soldier, the ponce from the dive, the negro. The soldier first, the negro last, But there's no-one up there now. So she stares down into the water, trembling slightly, at the same time slightly curious, and the water is grey, alarming, with the rain coming down. It's the last evening, her last evening on this earth, and it's the last evening's water. She trembles slightly, runs away, trembles, runs to the helm where nobody is standing now, and at that something goes through her, as though her limbs were sorting themselves out, and as soon as she is no longer confused or trembling she sits quietly down at the

[22] The Hannah Cash film. Perhaps the pirate film referred to on p. 60. The 'Ballad of Hannah Cash' is in *Poems 1913–1956*, p. 69, but only the name seems to relate.

helm, gazes forward where you can't see far now, and the ship rises and falls; this goes on a long time, for hours, hours, night comes and it rises and falls. You see it indistinctly, you see everything indistinctly, – it's swimming in something rainy, grey, alarming, the water is all around now. You can hardly see at all, just something grey, lost, shadowy; it goes up and down, and down and up . . .

I'm writing this beside her, and she is asleep.

Monday 21st.

I spent the whole of yesterday, Sunday, on the *Orange Eater*;[23] it's finished. Now I'm up to my neck in *The Mystery of the Jamaica Bar.* These plots are so bloody difficult, I always work on them walking but it makes me damned tired and then I give up and the film runs on. I'll find myself spanning the whole globe with all these films. And since yesterday Marianne has been here, looking like a Gauguin, laughing because she is going to have a child and otherwise smiling: 'Perhaps I'll go to the doctor because of my job, and I've patched things up with R. because I'll have to stay with him anyway till June because of the child; told him he's sexually abnormal and will never have anything to offer me.' And dizzy with films I meanwhile think 'She's wavering. She's not going to have it. I gave her her first sexual satisfaction. Romanticism erupted. She's not going to have it. And then she'll get old' – A child is something positive. But chains are oppressive and poverty can lacerate. And my hands are tied. At one point she's thinking 'I'll give it up'. Then 'I'll marry Recht'. And when she's lying with me she laughs. Says 'You can't live without me'. And 'Now I've got a child by you. Now you've got me.' And I think to myself: 'Tahiti'. I keep seeing water. And the child drowning in it. I only took her because she wanted a child. Now she's got to want it. I'll let her. No pushing now. No more trying to improve her. Am I her Redeemer? I'll help her. But I'm not sitting by her side in order to grow fat.

But however it turns out – I'm a small provisional point, a feeble affair that can't stand much and needs everything to be right for it, and I mustn't let myself get pinned down here by realities. They

[23] *The Orange Eater.* Is 'Der Brillantenfresser' in *Texte für Film I.*

can build twenty film factories round me just because now and
again the dove shits on my head, they can line the walls waiting for
me and sucking their thumbs; but I don't have to attend their
funerals in every cemetery in Europe, I don't have to wake
anybody up, and the frantic hooting of injured shareholders isn't
going to wake me from my sleep, nor does it prove anything about
my feebleness. I already have a child who is being brought up
among peasants, may it grow fat and wise and not curse me. But
now the unborn are competing for me ... To abandon everything
gracefully and wander off is all right if there's nothing one wants to
do better.

It's wrong to complain about Nature. Mount Gaurisankar[24]
isn't my enemy just because I'm unable to climb it. There are times
when it seems to me that the impulse with which I embrace life is a
feeble one and I only swim because I'm lying in the river. So I'm
washed along. I see a lot in the process, though.

> He who abandons the stars and spews out the earth
> Does not renounce
> The bitter taste
> Which is left.

Tuesday 22nd.
Munich. Klette. A grubby hundred-mark man. He accepts gifts:
percentages from the firm against whom he is supposed to be
representing his client, Otto's uncle. As a critic he gets 100 marks a
day for being an extra. As your agent he asks for fifty per cent. And
so on.

In the afternoon Marianne and I lay in the Griesle[25] Wild West.
The Maori woman among the brown Steppe grass, singing
Brahms's 'Feldeinsamkeit'. I don't know when I've heard more
beautiful singing. She might marry Recht. She's definitely going to
keep the child. I told her she should.

Now and again I get hungry for sentences that can be flung at
you, for the crazy delights of wordflesh and the cunning
allusiveness of the stage, I who am devastated by the cinema.

[24] Mount Gaurisankar. In the Himalaya.
[25] Griesle. Low ground bordering the Lech near Augsburg.

Wednesday 23rd.

Clear days. She is to have the child. Marry Recht. But at present I'm writing films, trying to provide a roof over her head. She says 'I'm like you. I've gone from one man to another. I'm a gypsy.' And she means 'I want a man who's different. One who'll hold on to me so I don't run away. Not a gypsy, you hear!' But I see it differently: she will have to learn to change. The only kind of hold is that exerted by a face. It's no real tie if it doesn't operate at a distance. It's no real love without counter-love. You can't hold on with your hands. A wooden roof: the rain will come through. And if it's not rain it will be something worse. Anyone who only wants to swim in the summer will find the water won't flow for him. And if someone wants to go under you can't hold him back. A good face is better than a good deed. Admittedly security is better than insecurity. But the only really secure thing is death.

Yesterday I collected her from the theatre. I was so tired I was ready to drop – from the film work – and I'd lain on her sofa in the afternoon, I was ready to drop, so I accompanied her to the tram; then she tried to haul me in, laughed, I felt the long, hot pressure of her slender hand, I shook my head, laughed, stood there, she drove off, I can still feel her hand's pressure. Today a messenger brought a letter: she is proposing to marry Recht, doesn't want to speak to me. A spirit of rebellion seizes me, I hesitate, choke it back, sit down and wait. Then I go on writing the film, that pointless film. She's got to come.

> But after that insult
> Heaped with accusations
> He laboriously went away
> And did not cleanse himself
> Nor raised his hand to ward off stones.
>
> No, the stones eased his going
> And he raised no hand
> And the insults seemed too few to him
> For now he knew
> What he was like.[26]

She hasn't come. I've done 100 shots, so the film is half finished.

[26] Poem not in the German collected edition of 1967.

The Orange Eater is entirely finished, 190–200 shots. Klette has promised 10 000 marks for the former, of which I may get 6000. And she hasn't come. I told her 'give me three months'. She's not giving me them. She's getting a roof over head, with that swine. Here am I already sawing the planks, working like a maniac, I'll have three films finished by next week, and she's getting married. Maybe I don't want to renounce Tahiti, maybe at some point she won't have a husband, but will she have a husband if she has Recht? As for the money, I'll be able to give it to her, won't I? All I can do is cover paper with writing. I'll spend four weeks doing all I can to save her, chasing round, begging, spending whatever I've got. She's simply running away.

This evening I was drinking with Cas and philosophising about whether one can scribble enough in four weeks to earn a thousand or two, the same kind of sum that a profiteer makes in a morning. Is a woman to be allowed to drift away because of a momentary money shortage which will be put right the next day, simply because she's frightened and wants to sleep in a lifeboat even though everything's perfectly all right. Of course I want Timbuctoo and a child and a house and no doors and to be alone in bed and to have a woman in bed, the apple off the tree and the timber too, and not to wield the axe and to have the tree complete with blossom, apples and foliage, all in close-up outside my window. Plus a man to dig in manure.

Thursday 24th.

Yesterday I drank four glasses of bitters and walked up and down outside Mar's house in the warm night, seeing no light behind the curtains. This morning I woke up feeling terrible, when there was a knock and in came Marianne, about seven o'clock, and fell on me. No, she was through with Recht now, she couldn't go on, she had been picturing how he would be to the child, her child, and she was so appalled she had to throw up and come over. That's all right: she wants the child. And I'll work, I must have faith in myself, perhaps I'll manage to sell my stuff, a lot of people do. And I just can't wait to have children. Timbuctoo is fine, and a child is fine too; you can have both. It'll be called Peter or Gise, no-one is going to murder her. Right. Then I shall work for Gise as best I can. And that's the best thing for the woman; that swine is no husband for her, and a child is the best thing in the world. I'll help her even if I don't marry her, for I am strictly provisional and need room to take off, I'm still growing.

Friday 25th.

'Under the sun of the Lech meadows'. Cas was there at one point. She was particularly charming. I am her husband, she lay in my arms laughing. She is around all the time. Overnight till the next morning. The maid opened the door and saw her in her chemise. I threw the red plush coverlet over her and over the bed, the maid walked through the room, I worked on *The Secret of the Jamaica Bar*. During today and tonight I've written nearly 80 shots.

Saturday 26th.

I'm living in luxury with the most beautiful woman in Augsburg, writing films. All in broad daylight, people stare at us. How long will it be before God's patience gives out and I'm sitting in the gutter being pissed on by dogs?

Crisis in the evening.

We were lying by the Lech this afternoon, Cas, M. and I, then M. went to the Aichers', I was to fetch her at 10, when Aicher appeared. 'Recht's here. He knows all about everything. M. can't come.' I wanted to go up, but she said it had all calmed down, he was going to keep M. for the night, they weren't going to see one another for a fortnight. I believed him, went to the 'Lamm' and waited. He promised me he would bring M. round next morning. About 11.30 I went round to his flat just the same, and whistled. M. threw the key down. Recht had spent hours looking for her this evening, being convinced that she hadn't spent the night in her own flat. She admitted she'd been with me, whereupon he beat her up, dragged her by the hair etc. She had big swellings: was quite confused. I took her away at once, we went to her place, she packed. Tonight the Flight into Egypt, prior to the Massacre of the Innocents . . .

Sunday 27th.

To Munich first thing. Kramer came too. Mar went to her parents, I shaved, she came back with Kramer, there was nobody at home. I went to see Dr. **Zoff** while Mar rested, utterly deadbeat, feeling worse and worse. I found a little dried-up brown man, with a shrivelled face like Beethoven's (authentic) death mask, and a quiet, wily expression; he told me to bring his sister along. I lunched with Mar, decided to polish off the novel, and drove with her to her brother's. We were walking up to the house when Recht arrived looking pale, lugged himself out of his car and came up to us perspiring coldly. 'Are you going to Otto's?'[27] She nodded. I walked coldly beside Mar, not looking at him. He lumbered awkwardly after us, breathing heavily. Then he asked to speak to me and I invited Zoff to be present. We sat in a big room. He wanted to do a deal, described the whole thing, his unease over the past months, his fears whenever he was being lied to. He's been her man for four years, he's been more to her than I realise – and than she does for that matter, in her currently rather confused state. I should go away for a fortnight to help clarify the situation. I asked him whether after that he would abide by Mar's decision: he said 'No. Never.' Then he started threatening me. I cut him off. 'That's your business. Let's drop it.' He shouted 'Right. Then to put it crudely, I'm supposed to make your bed for you, eh?' I said, 'No. You're to do nothing at all.' More threats: 'As for what I am going to do to *you*, that's another matter.' I said: 'Don't let's discuss that. Act.' I said, 'I have my rights. Sit down, I've got something to say to you.' He walked round me, went pale, squinted up at me. Knew what was coming. I said, 'She's going to have a child. She came the night after that scene at the station.' (She had already told him this ...) He flinched, went over to Zoff. 'What do you think of that?' Zoff remained seated, saying 'All very extraordinary...' Recht kept on rushing round, gesticulating: 'But it's just not possible. She had her period a week ago. She showed me the blood-stains on her nightdress. We had a quarrel about it.' (He had been unwell, had slept at her flat.) Then he asked me if he could speak to Mar. I asked her if she wanted him to, saying 'Do that'. Went out. When Zoff fetched me in again R. had been crying, he asked me to sit down and made a speech, really shaken. 'It was not granted to me to make this woman happy. It will be your task to do so.' He wanted me to promise to give her up if she ever left me as she was now leaving him. He held out his hand, I shook it. He took me by the sleeve and said. 'They say I'm a strong man in business, but where this woman is concerned, my heart is weak.' He had told her 'One can't be big *and* happy at the same time'. Then he went off. Marianne lay on the sofa. She had been crying. Tonight she slept at my place.

Tuesday 29th to Thursday 31st.
I once more told Marianne that I can't be married. She had been through a dreadful night during which she saw Recht's utterly desperate face and heard him saying 'What about those four years, were they absolutely nothing?' She said, 'I can't have the child outside wedlock', and once again started wondering whether she should keep it or not. She said 'Last night it seemed to me that I wouldn't after all be able to get away from Recht.' And with a sad expression (being depressed by my announcement) she told Aicher: 'It really is much harder than I thought.' And now Recht's non-stop flood of tears has begun swamping this town. On the second day he said 'When she comes back her child will be my child', and the whole municipal theatre knows the legend of the Noble Admirer. He has been running around like crazy, brimming with magnanimity, with the result that a whole procession of sympathisers has been turning up at Mar's, despatched by R. Starting on Saturday, **Heinrich Eduard Jacob**, a Jewish literary gent; Monday, R. Aicher, actor; then a varied assortment consisting of Mar's mother (he kissed her hand, sobbing), Schelz, theatrical agent, Schreiber, associate. But Mar makes mistakes. She took the 1000 marks which Recht gave her brother, she promised Schreiber not to see me for five days. She accepted Recht's flowers, and she's thinking it over. R. meanwhile writes her that miracles may last for three days but his love is for ever. And that he'll hack off his left hand, the one he maltreated her with.

APRIL

Friday 1st to Sunday 3rd.
At noon to Tutzing with Mar. Stayed at the 'Seehof' till Sunday.
She frequently felt sick but calmed down. The thought that
plagues her is that she has got no home. She can't go on living in
lodgings. So she's glad to be at her mother's just now. Somehow or
other she imagines she can live with Recht, though not as his wife;
and even though she won't admit anything else she tells me her
mother said (had to say?) that you don't get away from the man
you have had a child by. But the child has been saved, that is the
positive achievement of these few days.

Monday 4th.
Munich. Otto came to Tutzing[28] as my case has not been
postponed.[29] I've spent today chasing around collecting de-
positions: Feuchtwanger good, as always, Sinsheimer[30] wrote
something against his better judgement, Kutscher[31] was evasive.
    Visited Mar at her parents'. She has been mooching around the
house feeling sick most of the time. At my place this evening we
came close to missing the train, because I took her suddenly on the
sofa, and she was marvellous: fresh, gay, loving. Then the train to
Augsburg. She slept on my shoulder. Otto collected me. He's
found a lawyer etc. I escorted Mar home. Possible engagements in
Wiesbaden, Stuttgart, Mannheim. She wants to go to Stuttgart
tomorrow. I tumbled into bed.

Tuesday 5th et seq.
She has accepted Wiesbaden for September at a salary of 10,000
marks. That will do to buy soap with, the currency there is based

[28] Tutzing. On the Starnberger See.
[29] Vera-Maria Eberle, of the Augsburg municipal theatre, was suing Brecht for
libel on account of a review of Hebbel's *Judith* in the left-wing *Augsburger
Volkswille*. A settlement was reached on 12 April.
[30] Sinsheimer. Not identified.
[31] Kutscher. Arthur Kutscher, 1878–1960, Professor at Munich University,
friend and biographer of Wedekind, teacher of a famous seminar on criticism and
the drama attended at various times by Johst, Zarek, Brecht, Klabund,
Warschauer, Hedda Kuhn (of those mentioned in the Diaries).

on the Franc.[32] Hagemann[33] will chuck her out if she's pregnant, he's another pig, as she well knows. She has begun calculating again: end of this week. Continually seasick, hypnotised by her brilliant career like a chicken by a chalk line, pushed by mother and father, nudged in the ribs, she has gone back to imagining what it would be like if she visited the doctor. The phrase 'success at all costs' has once again cropped up; Hagemann is interesting, a gentleman, might fall seriously in love, that way lies her career. She said 'You're too young. You go on the swings. You're not someone one can marry.' The Aichers, having got a job in Vienna, are tempting her like harpies, ardently chanting the attractions of grand opera. Mrs. Aicher tells her 'He's a lover. He's no husband.' She listens to it all. Keeps thinking about it, sails from Augsburg to Munich and back, eats in small inns, is continually seasick, the papers are full of wonderful things about her Dorabella. While she packed I sat and smoked, cracking jokes and looking benevolently at her; does she realize how Recht has spoiled her, she has become absolutely helpless. For him of course she was an idol, something from another planet, a showpiece, he kept her on an altar, but he loved her unattainability and handed her over, slavering, to the harpy. In the end I saw that it was a matter for her of wife or cocotte, that vanity is greater than any upheavals and that R. is standing at the end of the road (downhill); so I brutally denounced child murder. Little by little she is coming round to the idea of having the child on her own. That's where I want her. The doctor disappears through a trapdoor, the parents get telegrams (in lieu of a visit), the subject is filed away.

Tuesday 12th.
The Mystery of the Jamaica Bar is finished and with Klette. Ditto *The Diamond Eater*. Kiepenheuer and Cassirer[34] have turned down *Baal* (no stage rights). The Eberle case continues. In the afternoon Mar and I were in the Siebentischwald, the trees are getting green, she was wonderful in the grass, people could watch us, it really was worth seeing. On the way back Beelzebub joined us. It emerged

---

[32] The Franc. Wiesbaden was in the French occupation zone.
[33] Dr Carl Hagemann, director of the Wiesbaden state theatre from 1920–30.
[34] Kiepenheuer and Cassirer. Two leading Berlin publishers. The former finally published *Baal*, also Brecht's *Versuche* 1930–33.

that R. had had her once again at the beginning of February, 'a kind of rape', and that at the time she thought for an instant he might give her a child. Since then she had never been his, but she went on sleeping with him and he still practised perversions on her. That was before her second period, and was 'utterly unimportant'. All the same she was lying that time when she said she had fought him off; in fact he had been wholly in her and she was disgusted by him. Everything had turned green by now, we slowly walked through the mild twilight, it was more depressing than anything she has done (which is saying a good deal), and she's as smooth as a pebble on the riverbed. I went off sadly, joined **Walter**[35] and went to a little philistine rumpot called Helm, an engineer who raves about Goethe and floats his ideals on strings like kites; extricated myself around 2 a.m. and walked to the infantry barracks, where I regretted that I hadn't stayed with her, and whistled for all I was worth. No sign of a light.

Wednesday 13th.
Spring is here, I'm doing nothing and am still on my own with Mar. But there's also the unsettled business with Bi, and this is a 15-inch gun that could score a hit amidships, except that the sea is still heaving, yo ho ho, and it's impossible to aim; but I'm waiting for the detonation or anyway for the wind to drop. Because I asked Bi if she would marry me, and she said in three or four years. And her cousin arrived while I was with her, about 9.30 a.m. and she sent him away without letting him in and didn't want me to know who it was. Because I had said I didn't like men calling on her. So I told her she didn't love me any more because nowadays she was always wanting her freedom and not wishing to obey me any longer and I told her all right, I'd let her go. But then she wrote a letter saying she couldn't make the break, she realised that she was not right for me as she was and would like to spend half a year on her own trying to become like she used to be. At that I wrote to her that I loved her and would wait. And she wrote to me that she needed a bit of time and would meanwhile be faithful to me.

Around midday I went to her place and it was bad, and I was full of misgivings, and after that I took her on the sofa and hurried to

[35] I.e. Walter Brecht.

the station. The train had gone, so I met her in the evening, we walked to the cathedral square, she had talked to Recht, told him she'd marry him if he'd stop bothering her. Which he promised he'd do. When I heard this I felt a small thin stiletto pierce my chest, and then she said she had told him she would always be my wife even if we never saw each other again, as this was probably what I'd want as soon as I heard what she'd told him (that she wanted to marry him). And at that I looked at her, got up and walked away. I went home, then went back again to the square, where I had left her still sitting with so desperate an expression on her face. But she wasn't there, so I went to the Lech, then it struck me that she must be at my place, and I went home. Then Walter told me 'Miss Z is upstairs', and I went up, and there she was sitting crying and said 'Hold me. I can't live without you. Why am I always doing the wrong thing?' And her whole body trembled, so that I put her to bed and she stayed till the morning.

Thursday [*14th*].
Munich. Klette has been trying to sell the *Diamond-Eater*. Went to a café with Bi in the evening. She was nice, serious and intelligent. I loved her, I kissed her in the bushes. Then I travelled home. (We are going to wait.) Mar in the night, tired and seasick, said she had spoken to R. and all was well.

Friday [*15th*].
In the morning I roughed out the whole of a film comedy (*Lovematch*[36]), then at midday I met R. at Mar's. I heard calm voices when I was still outside, went in and found them unpacking, she has moved one floor up. R. said Mar was still unclear about many things, she must be given time. Neither he nor I should take any steps. Mar didn't say much, just that she *was* clear but R. brushed it off. I talked about books and left. Mar walked down the stairs with me, looked amazed, then came to the Kraal with me. I gave her a pretty brutal account of what she was doing, running around like a drunken schooner. She had felt sorry for him, he's diabetic, looks like death, of course he didn't have to come every day, not just yet anyhow ... I'm starting to regard this sort of thing as infantile and told her I won't have it. I laid down what I want.

---

[36] *Lovematch*. No trace remains.

Saturday [*16th*].
Spent three hours talking to R. We walked up and down the avenue again and again, he wept, he pleaded. He had wanted to conquer the world, he was confident he could take on all comers, even if he went blind, if he went bankrupt: but he can't lose this woman. He is diabetic, 4.4%, he'll soon be dead, these are his last months, is his corpse then to lie across Marianne's threshold? She is to go off with him somewhere for four weeks, she has promised to. One must allow her her freedom, she's marvellous, infallible, a mature woman, he still hoped she hadn't finally closed the chapter marked R. I walked beside him saying virtually nothing, dry, sober. He compared me to Robespierre, the 'pedant of liberty'. Come to that, I didn't make difficulties; I'm sorry for him as long as his froggy fingers don't touch me. He says 'dear friend', he weeps in public, he's more magnanimous than an archangel, he beats God for virtue and the devil himself for tenacity. At the same time he's clever as only a Jew can be and has the morals of a horsethief. I wasn't shocked, simply embarrassed. He's so old. So worn out, slimy, miserable; he has the effrontery to try to scare me with the stink of his putrefying corpse, to bother me with his self-abasement; he heaps his worries about himself on to me, and his tactics are no better than his actual rights.

In the evening I made him come to see Mar, who felt ill, was having pains but had none the less dragged herself to the telephone for fear I mightn't come any more. She told him she didn't want to see him till further notice; he was gentle and gave in, and she was glad everything was all right.

Sunday [*17th*].
Very early in the morning Lud and I travelled out to Paar.[37] I chased around for six hours looking for a place for Marianne. Lud explained Fletcher's system[38] which he has adopted. On my return a great row with Papa, the Eberle woman having published the settlement, which looks disgraceful; I just hadn't paid attention in court, wanting only to win time. Then to Marianne, who had

[37] Paar. A river some six miles East of Augsburg, flowing north-east to join the Danube at Ingolstadt.

[38] Fletcher's system. A theory of mastication propounded by a doctor of that name.

performed last night without having consulted her doctor (as I'd asked) and was once again having pains. She told me she had been to Maxim's with her parents, had talked to R. ('a few words'); she found him more and more dislikeable. (She realised, as she said this, that she'd behaved badly.) Something broke. I yelled I'm definitely going away, I'm fed up; if you can't free yourself, stay there. She said I must have patience, at which I told her mine had run out. After that I regretted my outburst, she's unwell, I sent her upstairs. I behaved wrongly, and so did she. I'm tired of all this, though.

Monday [18th].
I'm sick of all this. The whole business is wearing me down. The cinema lays me out, my enemies dig me in. What am I supposed to do with this pregnant woman? I'd like to be good to her. The blows are coming too thick and fast. Now she's spending the day in bed, but the conductor is bringing her a new part, and the harpy is smiling at her. I meanwhile go on reckoning: once I get some money I'll do this and that, build castles in the air, wallow in banknotes, make complicated calculations. She laughs at that, she just lives for the moment, but I have to spur myself on to make money or I shan't want to. The days are grey, my stock stands low. There are moments when I have no feelings whatsoever about this woman. Bi still remains closer to me, I keep on trying to work out how I can get out of this, return to her, and then I go on totting up my fabulous figures: *Diamond Eater* 10,000, *Mystery* 5000, *Lovematch* 5000, *Drums* 50,000, Prize film[39] 5,000. But Mar actually wants to send her sister to Merano as soon as I've got the money, fancy that!

Tuesday 19th.
There were moments when all he could think of was flight. The trees were turning green and he had lain horizontal on his bed. The best part of it had been his idleness, oh what fat thoughts he had, what angels and devils of thoughts! The dreamer turned into a calculator, and hesitation became a prop to the hesitant. (David.) Once, years earlier, he had nearly achieved his breakthrough, in the

---

[39] 'Prize film'. No trace remains.

days of Absalom's insurrection when he was sitting on the wall. For two days he sat in the sun not sleeping during the intervening night, and he was within a hair's breadth of becoming silent. But that evening Uriah the hesitant came to him and he was not able to last out, but took himself off once again.

Am in Munich. I'd heard that Bi (and her sister) had been sitting in the Orchideengarten with a musician one evening; she had lied to me saying she was going to the Ludwigsbau, and had let him pay for drinks and a car. He's a ghastly fellow. Bi was alarmed, she is sad ('to be always having this kind of unpleasantness'), she's looking forward to Kimratshofen. I couldn't sleep at night; I'd realised 'this is amidships for me, don't shoot!' She's worth more than everything else to me; when I wake up she's my wife, I'm never certain of her, she has a stronger hold on me than all the rest, it's her I love. I go off home, my mind halfway at ease, after being good to her. Henceforward I shall give credit all round and make as few demands as possible.

Wednesday [20th] to Saturday [23rd].
The above actually took place on Wednesday morning. In the a'noon Marianne and I went to Burgadelzhausen near Paar. The little room was cold and draughty, the food good, but (first rate) pork as always; now it rained, now the sun came out, the whole time it was cold and Marianne felt seasick. I smoked, ate, slept with her in the big room, lay on the grass with her, she's thinking of marrying R, having all her children by me. No, she's not like Bi, she can't really be here on her own, the peasants will laugh at her, the room won't do. I'm stacking her away among the rats, bedding her in manure, slowly feeding her to death with pork. I'm a scoundrel. On the Saturday we had a $1\frac{1}{2}$ hours' drive in the butcher's cart to Paar, I left for Augsburg, she for Munich to her mother's. I've been thinking a lot about Bi, she noticed that. But once I was rolling along in the train with the rain coming down I smoked a cigar and felt content to be rolling, without any identifiable wishes and with no complaints. I'm satisfied with rain and insecurity, hunger and responsibility, I'll accept any challenge, my line is – rolling. That was a good quarter of an hour, it gave you something to hold on to in the shifting scene, as do friends' faces and nothing else.

Sunday [24th).
On my own once again. Cas dragged me round the art gallery, which always makes me laugh, Otto filled me with coffee, it rained, and in the mist things seemed to be sorting themselves out. The trees are green, there'll be a wedding this autumn, and before that the christening. The father's a genius, the child is lying in fresh linen, Tahiti is a beautiful part of the world. The cinema's being recalcitrant; if it yields milk Bi will be going around in pyjamas. Who wants to know what's better?

A little longer, and I'll be lying in the grass ... [It's raining on the fresh leaves, but that doesn't stop them screaming in the rowing boats on the lake. I had coffee with Heigei, now I'm going to play the guitar with Hartmann. That's the way it goes.

Monday 25th.
Munich is devouring films. I was at Marianne's, she was lying down seasick, woke up; Recht took her to Frankfurter's,[40] he gave him 2000 marks, she must get married, then Wiesbaden would be a certainty. The harpy too is beckoning the expectant mother. Her career leads over children's corpses into the public mortuaries. The novel called *Her Last Chance* or *Beggar's Rags Or Laurel Crown*? is reaching its final pages, which are badly printed and full of mistaken prophecies. True, she dragged me into Recht's room, on to his ottoman, but on Sunday R. talked for hours on end and in the evening he talked some more and she promised to marry him. I went with Bi to see the dancer von Schrenck,[41] whom both of us liked, then we spent some time in the café and I was good and affectionate to her, turning back to her, and she went out of her way to be nice.

Tuesday 26th.
In the morning went with Klette to the Bavaria Studios. Seitz[42] was directing a load of old rubbish with 15,000-mark extras. This is where the scum collects, people with remnants of old make-up instead of faces. This art has its roots in the kitchen sink. After that

[40] Frankfurter's. Eugen Frankfurter, a theatre and opera manager.
[41] Edith von Schrenck, a dancer.
[42] Seitz. Franz Seitz (the elder), film director.

M. sat at my place and we had further revelations. She had gone to the theatre with R. and Frankfurter on Sunday. Etc., etc. I told her: 'Him or me.' She said 'You.' She promised to tell him she would never, never marry him, etc. I said 'I'm no gigolo.' She began to feel very ill. She stayed the night. We slept too. In the early morning we made love like horses. It is all right, and as I was leaving she wrote down 'I have promised him...' Then I went. She presumably went on lying there: her father fetched her home.

Thursday 28th.
Sailed off to Kimratshofen with Bi. It was raining on the way there. Wind blew. The woman brought our little boy. I was profoundly happy. I'd been frightened he might look like a peasant. He is slim, with delicate limbs and a fine clear face, curly red hair but smooth in front, he's lively and has big dark brown eyes. He likes a joke, laughs a lot, keeps running around and playing with a whole succession of things; but he's never violent and never noisy, just friendly and gentle all the time. He hardly says anything, but he plays in an original way (he put my hat on a toy horse) and gives away everything he gets to all and sundry. He took hardly any time to get used to me, played with me and ran towards me rather than towards Bi, who didn't immediately strike the the right note, and thereafter left him alone rather than risk a rebuff. I lent him my hat, then my tie, my watch, ten pfennigs. I shall ask Papa if he can have him to live with him. – Bi is nice, and I like her.

Friday 29th.
At midday Bi and I went to Augsburg. It was raining.
    Nothing is so sad or so disturbing as sitting in dark rooms, specially when there are a number of them and they are totally quiet. But it's never so horrible as when you've been bawling for some time at the top of your voice and indulging yourself in sinful chords on the guitar, then you fall silent and get feelings of revulsion and afterthoughts, like a dog gets worms. Doubtless nobody is guilty, particularly if they are helpless, and who is going to bawl out a pregnant woman because she wants a roof over her head? What binds her to R. is the nasty side, his feminine, canine character; she can't stand his trickling away without her, for what attracts her is the calmness of an open drain. In the process she has

slowly, bit by bit, been losing her self-confidence, because whichever way she turns she can see nothing but setbacks and losses. All the same, if she too floats away, festooned with shit and decay so that her face becomes unrecognisable, it will be a bad summer with her on board; for there was nothing more I could say to her when she left me; and this chokes me just as though she had taken something away with her.

Saturday 30th.

It's a damned novelette, and whatever swansong may be heard above the treetops the struggle down below is for extremely tangible things. These people go bankrupt because they're insufficiently acquainted with their own faces: they forget how brutally clearly the main outline will in due course emerge, running as it does from negligence through stupidity and petty impatience. The harpy still haunts her. R. brings her to heel, flatters her that her talents are too big for bourgeois life (to which she herself adds that she can't live in poverty, having found herself unable to do so in her present sick and pregnant state). But I told her 'If there's anything there you can transgress against it. What, shield the delicate plant from the slightest breath of wind? You should be able to rise to the top with *two* children. Why rate yourself so low? Do at least marry a multi-millionaire. But once you're in labour, let me tell you, my hand will mean more to you than all the applause in Wiesbaden. To get satisfaction out of art you need to make art with your body and soul, and you need to have your body and soul in order to do this.'

Last night she arrived with Otto and spent the night, and promised she wouldn't marry; she couldn't exist without me, she said, weeping. And went off the next morning intending to make an appointment with Recht for midday in a café, and at midday along came R. with a letter from her: she was going to marry R. So I went off and dictated a letter to her, a note saying that she was pregnant with my child and was abandoning me although I had asked her to stick with me till it should be born. She wrote stiffly, and cried and took my hand, and I gave it to her and left.

MAY

Sunday 1st.   *Anniversary of Mother's death*
Once again Manitu is left alone in the cloud. No longer is the white
squaw heard singing across the waters, no longer does Manitu
make speeches into the wind ... The squaw has gone downstream,
and his child is within her. The spring begins, green is the tree and
the rain washes away the dirt. Once they lay in the fields, often in
bed, and altogether in five different places. While it was winter she
went with Manitu, she was still deceiving him in the springtime,
and ere summer had come she went with the fat man who fed the
harpy. The child that sees his face will get his eyes, and its mother's
corpse when it comes back from the harpy. The squaw will weep
into the wind and run after Manitu who once made speeches into it.
And the films are shown in the dark; as the grass was growing the
horse died.

Monday 2nd.
The days are spewed-up empty plum skins. It's raining gently, a
wind has got up, the room where I am sitting is cold. I keep seeing
the Maori woman beside her fat financier, and although I am quite
cold and without any desire I'm still sorry for her, because she is
doing something wrong and cannot endure it. But alongside my
fear that she may come back once she has got herself into a
complete mess I feel an increasing contempt for her. And on her
wedding day I shall pluck her out of me by the roots as the old
whore she has once again become.
    I am good to Bi and support her. Can't do any work.

Tuesday 3rd to Friday 6th.
Now for retribution and purgatory. Bit by bit I drag a dreadful
story out of Bi. She has been corresponding with a café violinist, a
slimy fellow, and he kissed her and she visited him and lay in his
bed. She never gave herself to him, that's clear from the letters.
She's very sorry, but in her view he's an uncorrupted idealist. The
days when she's lying are hell.

Saturday 7th.
Last night I dreamt about He; she had grey hairs across her

forehead and I was only surprised once she had gone. And I had forgotten the dream when I found a little lump on my penis which reminded me that she once dreamed I had caught syphilis. Dr. Hirsch at the clinic of course said it was a herpetic blister, nothing special. All the same early in the morning I was worried, and I was just waiting for Mar, who had called yesterday on Heigei and on me, only I wasn't at home. Then her sister turned up instead: Mar had begun haemorrhaging last night, though she had not yet lost the child. They were unlikely to save it. I was alarmed for her, because it could be her eternal damnation, and I wrote her a line to calm her down. But she didn't want me to come because R. mightn't like it. Heigei went, we were thinking of an abortion, he suggested E [...]⁴³ as a good doctor, she agreed. And on the medicine bottle was written 'Mrs. Recht'. I was appalled at the failure of her theft and that she should abandon my child because her heart was not pure. But I've ceased to love her, am just coldly observing. I have been spending a lot of time with Bi, whose distress has made her thinner so that she has now become childlike and beautiful, and a truth once more: I love and respect her. And I went on the swingboats with her at the Au fair.⁴⁴

Sunday 8th.
It's a peaceful day: sunny with no people about. In the morning I wandered around among the green vegetation, which is new to me. Then Lud came and played Bach and I made tea, both of which were equally valuable activities. Of course nothing matters all that much. Here is a pregnant woman running away, and even if I don't know why, I know she was good when she was there, and she sang beautifully, particularly at dusk ('Wenn mein Schatz Hochzeit macht, hab ich meinen traurigen Tag' – Mahler). But we like to see everything from a single standpoint, and imagine that deeds are worth more than a face. Instead of rejoicing when for once somebody doesn't deceive us, and declaring a general amnesty for all deceivers. And so we want all our work to be good so that once we're living in Tahiti we can say: 'It was all good.' But it's Tahiti that stops it from being good, my friends...

⁴³ E[...]. A deliberate editorial omission from the German text.
⁴⁴ Au. Munich district on the right bank of the Isar.

Monday 9th.

Extraordinary how sensitive I've grown in the course of this last quarter's circus. At noon I was walking to the station, steadily slowing down, and smoking, but like a man on his deathbed, and I was just making up my mind to go and get drunk when R. plucked me by the sleeve. He looked white as a sheet and avoided my eyes. And he said that Marianne had again lost a lot of blood on Saturday and they'd operated on her, also Dr. W[. . .][45] had been there (who induced her abortion the time before). 'More or less accidentally', said R. And I'd not been wanted ... But R. had spent the whole night by Marianne's bedside. And so the good fairies turned their backs on Marianne Zoff, who started by running around and ended up with a child's little body in the slop-pail. She was not to have a child, the whore; my child went from her because her heart was not pure.

I tottered home as if I had been struck on the head. To experience such baseness! I could strangle that tart. It's the filthiest thing that's ever happened to me, not that I claim to be an expert. I've told her a thousand times 'You can't do that. Not *you*.' This is the reward. Now she can go down the river, *without* ballast. *That's* what she wanted. All the rest was attitudinising under the spotlights to café music. *That's* what she *really* wanted. I've never seen the whole swindle of whoredom – romanticism – so nakedly. The pregnant whore unloading. And this is the leaky pot, with every man's discharges trickling into it, that I wanted to instal in my rooms. Hence her frantic fear of being abandoned, seen through, unmasked, abandoned, her desperate hope that a new, unprecedentedly powerful situation could be created to wrench, extricate, wheedle her away from whoredom. Pluck her out of me! Out! Out! Now let her be used as a whore, thrown to other men, left for R. to have. Now, just as she's about to say 'now it's all settled'. And under this flag she can henceforth cruise the oceans as she likes, because she's really too mean and cowardly to put up with what she herself is doing. She wasn't even prepared openly to acknowledge her best deed, no piece of meanness was too dirty to cloak her, that bad actress who never plays herself but always some other better performer, in other words one who is liked better by the mob.

[45] Dr W[. . .]. A further editorial omission.

These days I am entirely on my own, and a good thing too. After Marianne I shall have to be very careful about making generalisations for a while. In the evening I walked by the Lech, smoked and pulled myself together. I thought about *Galgei* and all the rest, about Frank too. At night I've been sleeping badly, as if I'd committed a murder.

Tuesday 10th to Saturday 14th.
M[unich]. Paid one visit to Marianne in her nursing home. She wept, I said all I had to say, buttoned up to the neck; she ripped it open, clung to my knees, wept. In two months' time she will come, she wants to be free till then. Cruelly I showed her the photos of Frank, she wept loudly and I pitied her. But then I went away without difficulty, and the days will engulf her.

I've been spending a lot of time with Bi, who is once more good and loving, as I am too. All the same she lied to me yet again, went to a café one evening with some clodhopper from Kimratshofen, and I caught her scurrying away unobtrusively, the stupid cow. I told her I had kissed Mar two or three times in the snow in the Siebentischwald one evening: that's as far as I dared go, since she went absolutely white.

Meanwhile Reicher[46] has sent back the *Mystery*. And because the days are turning warm and green I don't care a damn about most things and have made up my mind to improve myself.

Whit-Sunday 15th.
The weather's sunny, I've been wearing my good blue suit and walking about like a sailor ashore; smoking, spitting in the eye of any thoughts of mine I run across, and never feeling completely at home in my old skin. I'm reading Gaston Leroux's *Mystery of the Yellow Room*, a first-rate detective novel, the sort of thing I love: ingenuity served up like the Baptist's head (chopped off), and I'm not entirely content but keep niggling at various 'improbabilities' like a big fool. Somebody spitting into my enjoyment. When I spit at something I forget my hands are in my pockets and it's as if the spit were on a string; I keep pulling it back. I've been on at Father repeatedly about taking in Frank, pointing out the number of empty rooms, just like a hotel, the trees in the garden that nobody

---

[46] Ernst Reicher of the Stuart Webbs company.

climbs, and all that. But he won't bite, and I get depressed, begin to feel ashamed. Marie Roecker's been putting him against it, if only by her expression and her way of coming in whenever I'm talking to Father. I hear all her arguments served up by him. In the old days I always stuck up for her when Mama, Walter and Father too were against her. Now she's dissuading Father from taking in my child because it would be such a nuisance. And Father himself starts saying that he's old and that these women are more than he can cope with and he's no longer all that keen on helping me. Also he's thinking of remarrying and has already started slowly ridding the house of us. And here am I with my hands among papers or in my pockets, scribbling stuff no-one will buy, smoking, thinking about my child and not earning anything. Just loafing around.

Whit-Monday 16th.
The days are filled with the twittering of birds. I'm slowly surfacing, but am leaky still. I know no restrictions. At the moment I'm pregnant with schemes for handing Frank over to Marianne. Politics again ...

The second day of the holiday. Cas and I walked by the Lech in the morning; we discussed *Galgei* and decided that a certain calm vision needs to be shown taking shape *above* the whole play, while the individuals ought to be characterised only by their relations with one another. In the afternoon Hartmann read me the Jesuits' conflicting views about the various permissible forms of sexuality. Here we see a mirror image of human sinfulness. The church's demands are precisely those of the megalomaniac and simultaneously fear-crazed animals that they are never able to satisfy. It is a systematic conspectus of all that they cannot tolerate.

At night to the municipal gardens, where we crawled around like Ichthyosauruses, absurdly unpopular.

Tuesday 17th.
Blue days. We lie – usually as a trio – in the army swimming school's water. Otto's sole way of paying for such pleasures is by impertinence. After a day spent without work, sated with smoking, gossiping, mooching around and useless posing, I sleep badly in the heat of my room and envelop myself in spasms of jealousy. Above the white ceiling floats Bi's face, restless.

Wednesday 18th.

Of all the arts that of writing is the vulgarest and most ordinary. It is too public, too unambiguous and open to checking. Even the most fertile thoughts are resumed by it in such a way that *eo ipso* they become flat and unpromising. The writer's own views lie plainly visible as does his wish to force them on the reader. There are no secrets, and where there are no secrets there's no truth either.

Thursday 19th.

She was here yesterday. Today she came again. She sent a messenger to enquire after me, and stood in the door swaying, pale as a corpse. She smelt of powder, and possibly this was to win my sympathy (for she had sunk with all hands, retribution had descended on her) or because of the rivalry with Bi, which is new. After she had gone off she told me in a letter that she was marrying R.; would I come. But I wasn't having any. Now she hurries round here on her first day. (And to think that once she shook her head over Sophie Barger.[47])

I had no time to explain everything. I had decided possibly to hand Frank over to her and keep her till the end of the summer. I hinted at this, then let her go, as usual. She said she was quite certain I ought to allow her time, and this I was doing. But I had told her that I wasn't her gigolo, and this had cut her to the quick. (It has already struck me more than once that everything might have turned out differently if I hadn't satisfied her that Friday night[48] when she arrived with Otto. She went away content and sold me down the river. According to our calculations that was the day the child died.)

Friday 20th.

Meier-Graefe[49] says of Delacroix that here was a warm heart beating in a cold person. And when you come down to it that's a possible recipe for greatness. It's our bad luck that we Germans

---

[47] Sophie Barger. The girl in scene 4 of *Baal*, who is fascinated by the poet and follows him across the countryside.

[48] that Friday night. I.e. 29 April.

[49] Julius Meier-Graefe, 1867–1935, leading art historian and critic, founder of the review *Pan*.

treat application and effort, even precision, as attributes of mediocrity (contemptuously known as 'promise'). This philistine attitude flourishes even among artists, which gave it a certain justification in this country thanks to the anxieties of the eminent. Where in Germany can you find that serious, frequently sober devotion to an idea coupled with an equally frequently fanatical devotion to a craft such as can be seen, for instance, in France (in the work of Van Gogh, Flaubert, Gauguin, Maupassant, Cézanne, Zola, Baudelaire, Stendhal, Delacroix)? The best works of our time are doomed to pass away thanks to their lack of any ethical approach on the technical side.

Saturday 21st.
Yesterday Marianne was here again, Otto too. She had told R. she wanted my child, and he was appalled and refused to permit it. She said she knew he hadn't changed, and that his only object was the prospect of no longer having to bother (i.e. marriage). But in fact he did succeed in talking her out of that. He is a squalid cripple, a female comedian, a brutal tyrant, and he's going to win because he stakes everything, stakes all this, and I stake nothing. That's to say he's going to win her dead body; and at the same time is going to profane it. I don't care what she does with him so long as he doesn't have her. He'll pay, slave away, may even be good, so long as he isn't allowed to exact payment, to enslave her and make her bad. He'll kiss her feet or trample on her face, depending on how she treats him. If he has to talk she won't have to listen, if he says 'home' she'll have to understand 'cage' or 'sty', because a home is simply people's environment, that's all. In one respect I underrated him: he really does know her. He knows all her weak points and how helpless she is against brutalities, and mercenary if it's in church, and mistrustful of her own body. It's only her weak points that he's intimate with, and the only characteristics of her that he doesn't notice are those against which he can do nothing. But one thing I see now: that she's doomed to end up in utter squalor as the romanticism is stripped from her, the great excuse of confusion taken away, and she herself goes to the bottom for no other reason than her squalor.

One of the cruellest and chilliest arguments to be brought against any given thesis is the usefulness of that thesis to the man propounding it. Admittedly, his self-interest should be allowed for; however, this has to be carefully checked, since even bribed judges can sometimes give correct verdicts. Any confusion of pedagogical aims with the expression of opinions about irreversible truths is extremely dangerous, yet it can be subject to proof if only, e.g., it can be established that one thing is truer than another, but *not* that one thing is true and another false. Hard as it is, it is essential when considering the possibility of eternal damnation carefully to dismiss all thoughts about its usefulness or otherwise from a pedagogical point of view. The best way of going about it is for me to say that *a priori* I consider this a pedagogically useful dogma, while being aware of the danger represented by my own opinion. For in fact nothing brings people so close to a state of eternal damnation as the conviction that there is no such thing. The majority of souls are lost not because people think the soul doesn't exist (theologically, if you like) but because they think souls are unloseable. Enchanted by the indestructible beauty of its own face, mankind cuts off its nose and thereby destroys what it considers beautiful. As for the reality of this dogma's existence, i.e. of its effects, the aesthete's demand of Nature – that mankind should itself own the whole range of possibilities from bliss to damnation – is balanced by a different demand, that aesthetics should be capable of covering this whole range, in other words that mankind should have the capacity to extract enjoyment from every kind of situation; and this second demand is supported by our actual will to live. This is the most important chapter of aesthetics and religion alike. Tragedy, which reproduces it in graphic images, appears to repose on the dogma of eternal damnation.

What I miss in *Galgei* is a character on the largest possible scale who can carry the story on his back. An infinite number of characters could be introduced into this story; I need the biggest. And he must be the one that places most obstacles in the way of the story and in no way gets exhausted by it. That's what's so difficult.

If one wanted to convey the Marianne business the thing that would need the most careful attention would be the unusual coloration of the setting. Here you have a woman whose family tree makes her an in itself perfect cross between Spanish aristocrats and Czech Jews, likewise a man who is half Jewish, half Czech (if

I'm not mistaken); and their story (since it may really be *their* story) unreels in a cool, more or less sober domain, which we might perhaps best bring to life by making it, say, the Black Forest. For the third participant, in whose domain it all takes place, is a much drier character, and this stubbornly militates against any romantic development of the narrative. This complication of the sightlines is further aggravated by the fact that the last-named is a littérateur, not so much with respect to his actions as where his attitudes are concerned. The half-Jew is a business man, the woman an opera singer, the young man a littérateur; the business man wishes to possess her mind, the littérateur her body; the business man is an idealist in words, a cynic in actions, the littérateur the reverse. The littérateur cuts a poor figure in this tale, because he does nothing and just because he is a littérateur. The business man a likeable one, because he is fighting for his life. The woman remains cloaked in darkness and can't herself see either.

What a colossal effort it can be to live, nothing more. And to hang coloured lanterns above one's decline. How evil life is and how severely one degenerates! To talk about one's sufferings and keep calm when evil occurs. The darkness of the all-eroding rain and the inbuilt torment of the pit ... In the evening one lies across the benches in the attitude of those who at one time used to pray. But there is no more grace, and the only answer is the hard silence of justice.

Sunday 22nd.
I've been smoking cheroots among the trees, trying to get Joseph Galgei in my sights. All I need is the haziest outline. He has a red wrinkled skin, particularly on his neck, close-cropped hair, watery eyes and thick soles. He seethes inwardly and cannot express himself. But everything derives from the fact that people look towards him.

Plans:
1. Write *The Plague Merchant* for **Granach**.
2. *Galgei* for the [Munich] National-Theater.
3. The pirate film for Mar.
4. *Summer Symphony* for Mar.

5. *Green Garraga* for the Kammerspiele.[50]

I recall a man in Amsterdam who could handle the heaviest iron weights with ease – with ease but not without bitter curses and a profound contempt for anything that looked like iron. If you took away this (fat) man's weights he relapsed into an utterly debauched melancholy, grew thinner (like ham hanging in a chimney) and lost his finest curses one after the other. What he missed was the sweat which the weights he'd been swinging represented; these constituted the basis of his contempt and the meaning of his existence.

On the way from Augsburg to Timbuctoo I saw Marianne Zoff
That sang in the opera and looked like a Maori woman
And was lovely in the grass, also in bed, and looked lovely in
  her clothes
And I slept with her too and gave her a child.
(She'd rolled herself in a ball like a hedgehog sleeping.
She was cunning as an animal and conducted herself without
  cunning.
She nodded her head when laughing, looked slantwise up at
  you and drew a blade of grass through her teeth
She walked from sheer joy
She once said to me: Chump!
She was proud of her legs.
She looked like scorched grass when passionate.)

[50] Plans. *The Plague Merchant* (*Pestkaufmann* or *Das Lazarettschiff*) was a scheme for a play set in South America. *The Green Garraga* too was to be set in Chile, according to the surviving MS of two scenes.

End of May to end of September 1921

MAY

Wednesday 25th.
I went to the lake with Bi. We lay in the green woods, had poppy-
seed cakes for tea, sunbathed in the boat; she looked incomparable,
slim and delicate. Then I showed her how to swim, as her 'face
keeps dropping into the water'. She soon picked it up after a bit of
floundering about.[1] In the hut we sat naked, she has so pure and
natural a style, an unparalleled charm and dignity in all she does.
We drank coffee during a fearful hailstorm (God was shooting at
the green bushes with bullets of ice as big as pigeon's eggs), then
did a film of [Schiller's] *The Maid of Orleans* in the gently dripping
woods. Bi acted the bit where Joan leaves the camp after the battle
and goes into the forest, where she once again becomes a little
country girl among the great trees; and she played it as naively as a
child and at the same time as artfully as a star. After all this time
she's still not exhausted, always full of surprises. She says I make a
manly impression when I talk, particularly my face, but much less
so from the back view, where I look irregular, small and slight;
that in bed I seem boyish and cheeky, and at my best when
something's happening. I love her very much.

Saturday 28th.
Otto and Cas have been wandering around the May festivities. On
one occasion Otto hauled me out, filled me with schnaps and
dragged me on to a farcical stage where I had to sing the
'Sentimental Song'.[2] I didn't know it absolutely by heart, and there
was a gent by the curtain who kept hissing 'Gestures!'; so I broke
down and staggered off with a lacerated conscience but some
applause none the less.

On Friday evening the Jörgen woman[3] visited me, and I laid the
foundations of my first billion. She has a patent cure for rough skin
on one's arms. I've got a mass of ideas in connection with
(animated) short advertising films. Her first step has been to take a
job in an occultist bookshop. She regards devotees of occult

---

[1] Interviewed fifty-six years later, Bi claimed that she could in fact swim but was
not sure that Brecht could.

[2] 'Sentimental Song'. I.e. 'Remembering Marie A.', *Poems 1913–1956* p. 35.

[3] Jörgen. Also mentioned on p. 59.

studies as promising clients. My job would be to believe in her. To believe in the billion, the patent cure and the lady. It's a piece of business like a thousand others. I love people who have ideas about conquering the world and start with skin cures.

When I let Marianne go I saw she was provided with credit. R. has taken the money off her (7000 marks) and now she's got to go back and earn some. She's sitting in Berchtesgaden and anything over and above what it costs her to eat she pockets. The whole family is there. I wrap myself in a smoke cloud and gloat to myself. Wait to see what she wants. Offer no opinion. But after spending two days down there she has written to say I should come, no-one would need to know, she'd bring me my meals every day. That rather damps my pleasure. I'd be put in the linen cupboard. Via the tradesmen's entrance. Into a marriage bed. 'The Master as Servant' or 'He's come a long way . . .'. I bluntly refused.

The rain has been drumming down on the leaves, the windowsills, the tarred streets. Earthly things are getting tedious. You infer them from the great thoughts, which are so simple. Women never reach further than their bed, they are not well directed, can't be sharply enough distinguished from one another, nor is their story carefully enough composed. They are either invariably the same and call for a lot of taste and imagination, or else they bore you by the mistakes they make about themselves, because they go on wearing these much too long, like underclothes. They'll change their underclothes, but not their mistakes. Of all the feelings with which love can entertain you the only one which isn't too utterly boring is jealousy. Moreover jealousy, which a man never catches from another man but always from a woman, provides your only chance of acquiring a favourable opinion of a man. Once anybody's feeling for literature is exhausted he is lost; since an educated person confronted with any sort of human situation will be interested solely in its literary packaging, its style, its ethics, the sharpness of its point or the brutality of its refinement. It would be better then to act stupid. Because it is pleasanter to see the greatest possible number of the cleverest and most imposing (i.e. decentest) possible people sweating away in an effort to abolish you than, forgotten by yourself, to become the most insignificant experience of four walls or a matter of embarrassment to a gutter-stone. It can be a laudable but by no means easily achieved undertaking to stage a small autodafé in the open, nor should you be so thoughtless as to think twice about putting yourself on the pyre if the little entertainment would otherwise be a flop. But people spare themselves and die of it. You must sacrifice your foot for the sake of your thigh and your thigh for the sake of your head. Generally however you only chase around because you're fed up with sitting, and then you get as many thoughts as a dog does worms.

Tragedy is based on bourgeois virtues, deriving its strength from them and declining with them. There is no sense in fumigating a saint if you believe in no gods at all. (Judas believing in the *Saint's* God is hard to take ...) As for comedy, in so far as it is profound and worth treating seriously, it tends to boil down to the worship of hangmen or doctors. Given one tiny touch of heroism the killing of a pig can spark off profound tragic emotions, while the sacrifice of an unimpeccable cow bereft of such (possibly deceptive) treatment cannot. To take a personal example, I'm not sure whether it's at all possible to convey the monstrous mixture of comedy and tragedy in *Galgei*, which lies in the fact of exhibiting a man who can be handled *in this way* and yet remain alive.

(Immortality through Incompetence; the Human Being Without a Heart ...) The theme of *Galgei* has something barbaric about it. It's the vision of a lump of flesh which whinnies uninhibitedly, and because it lacks a centre can endure any kind of alteration, like water flowing into any shape. The barbaric and unashamed triumph of meaningless life, running riot in all directions, using every conceivable form, neither having nor tolerating any reservations. Here you have a donkey living who is prepared to live on as a pig.

The question: Is he then living?

Answer: He is lived.

Sunday 29th.

I've got hold of G.K.C.'s detective stories.[4] The best I've yet read. Here the task really is performed by reason. These Englishmen may be patriots like Kipling or Catholics like Ch[esterton], but

[4] G.K.C. G. K. Chesterton, in whose 'Father Brown' stories the detective is a Catholic priest.

they understand their business and don't whittle away their problems but demonstrate the useful, practical aspects of their way of going about things, acting generally like those commercial travellers who sell thermos flasks by flinging their supposedly unbreakable wares on the floor with barbaric frenzy, or bashing them against other, more breakable models so as to demonstrate the merits of their own.

Now the Brown Spirit is sitting in solitude outside his wigwam, staring into the bushes. The wind is blowing and the bush is getting smaller and the squaw who has gone away is standing in the foaming white waters. If the buffalo keeps on running through the night it will take him seven days to reach the white waters, but it will take the waters a mere two days to reach the neck of the solitary squaw ... Nor does the Brown Spirit rise to his feet, for who is so swift as a buffalo? And the Brown Spirit blinks, for what is so deadly as the white water? And the bushes once more grow big ...

Psalm

We didn't bat an eyelid when the white waters rose to our
    necks
We smoked cigars as the dark brown evenings gnawed at us
We didn't say no when we drowned in the sky –
The waters didn't tell anyone that they were up to our necks
There was nothing in the newspapers about our not saying
    anything
The sky doesn't hear the cries of people who are drowning –
So we sat on the big stones like lucky people
So we killed the greenfinches which talked about our silent
    faces
Who talks about the stones?
And who wants to know what waters, evenings and sky mean
    to us?[5]

In the afternoon Cas and I talked about Marées.[6] He is like the littérateurs. A good decent workman, honest, talented, clean. But there's no metaphysics to his pictures. The perspective stops

[5] Translation by Christopher Middleton, reproduced from *Poems 1913–1956*, p. 76.

[6] The painter Hans von Marées, 1837–1887.

immediately behind the picture. What's there you can see; what he knows, is there. It is the most he can do. Not one picture is complete. There is no absolute, flawless creation, which can never be wholly exhausted, to back it up. He constructs his picture out of four or five elements. The picture is his discovery, not his vision. I respect engineers, I don't love them. Coldbloodedness is a miracle, it calls for heroism in the face of danger. Not so in the studio. Here a conquest is being planned. If M[arées] dispenses with philosophy his wooden dummies lack ideology and communicate no atmosphere. It is not effects that he renounces so much as their invention. Sound theory, rigorous limitation and ideological arbitrariness will in the long run always succeed up to a point, given a modicum of talent.

Monday 30th.
One should hit the nation in the heart. Every play a battle. Pursue one's development in the midst of a people. Exercise power. Or, like a Louis, just do everything provisionally? Be a golden demigod for a while, grinning above the tribes of monkeys? Withering with the green foliage, carried away into the woods by the wind? As he, the master, strides through the liana forest he ought to treat men like plants, slash them down, or like niggers with incomprehensible gurgling noises in their larynxes, understanding nothing but the whip. And when his grin wears off, he should finish up on a great rock, die like a plant, the one serious business on this planet, though not serious enough to be noticed.

To indulge in a simple narrative!

If only one could manage to see through walls and past the little people. And to glimpse the time that a thing has. One could prevent it from being brought to a stop.

'Seeing his attitude in the jungle you realised here was a soldier, he was big and agile and showed things his face (which was like a smooth stone washed out by river water). You could also see, specially from behind, that he was a mutineer, animals made a detour round him, he was the comrade of the men who had to shoot at him; a thing on his own, he lounged round the jungle with tobacco and gun, and whenever a bugle sounded he listened. He also slept in the open or at any rate left the doors open to see what might be coming up to him, and he slept with his cap on. He always walked in grass as tall as a man, though the tough stalks cut him so that he bled; he kept turning his ear in the direction of the wind, and on one occasion he was seen to shoot at a tree, at nothing but a green tree.'[7]

Talked to Cas about further paintings. I said 'The material must be right. Canvas, size, paint. No deceptions. No scattered patches that the eye has to try and bring together. Simple, strong colours. Three or four elements, carefully thought out, temperament well under control, see that the passion beats in great calm throbs.' Being strong on the emotional side just now he should restrict his effects to the purely painterly plane while choosing his subjects wherever he pleases. For instance the Maid of Orleans, i.e. a woman naked to the waist amid brown bodies of soldiers and with a classic transparent sky arching overhead. If it's to be theatre, let it be good theatre, respectable acting and no imitation of reality (rather, a precedent). I myself have a good deal of cultural awareness, and find the classical style 'refreshing'. We must get beyond baroque.

Tuesday 31st.
Have been reading Mauthner's *Last Death of Gautama Buddha*.[8] A first-rate book by that great writer. I shall get down right away to the history of atheism as soon as I've finished reading Meier-Graefe's *Delacroix* – profitably, I think.

---

[7] This passage relates to Brecht's first published short story, 'Bargan lässt es sein'.

[8] Fritz Mauthner (1849–1923), philosopher and journalist, author of *Der litzte Tod des Gautana Buddha* (1913) and *Der Athreismus und seine Geschichte im Abendlande.*

JUNE

Wednesday 1st to Friday 3rd.
At Starnberg with Bi, Otto, Cas. Much reading. Apart from that
I've just been wearing out my boots on the hot roads. It's no good
hurrying. The boat can run before the wind. I smoked a lot, sat in a
variety of positions, tried for a film in forty shots and wrote
Kiepenheuer a letter. Mar rang to say she'd like to come on
Monday, she sounded nervous but I was aroused by the sensual
note in her meaningless words. Every now and then I called on
Cas, who has been copying a Rubens, the play disgusts me, I keep
having to drink a schnaps to it. Have tried to interest Otto in rich
women, preferably married ones, who must provide capital for
films. God had his reasons for making him handsome.

Saturday 4th.
There are limits to everything. To what the woman does for her
man and the man for his woman. To what the father does for his
son and the son for his father: there are limits to it all. The son who
doesn't hit his mother deserves to have a monument put up to him.
The woman who doesn't deceive her man deserves not to have her
man tug her by the hair. The father who helps his son deserves to
go into the history books. I allowed the woman bearing a child of
mine to be hit. And the woman betrays me to whoever hit her. I
allowed my child to go among strangers. And my father doesn't
help me in my moment of greatest difficulty, and this pains me. My
mother frequently didn't love her mother; while I didn't tell my
mother that I loved her.
   My father invariably abandons me in times of peril. About the
Marianne business he believed a stranger, and wept in front of him
and betrayed me, holding me back so that my woman might be
taken from me. Never *once* did he ask after my child, never *once* after
the mother, though I told him that I wished to make her my wife.
He told me, with reference to the child, that he guessed 'I would be
able to fix things somehow or other'. So I mess around and incur
the worst sin of my life, which I know I shall not be able to bear. I
cook up films and fritter myself away. Things will soon have got to
such a pitch that I'll be chucked out of my house.

Monday 13th.
Once again it's all panoramic.

The colours in this country are bad. Everything's a grey, repeatedly thinned ink wash. On the rare occasions when they bring on a red moon one's not naive enough to keep calm. So at least the schnaps should be free. In a country with such colours the liquor ought to cost nothing.

Marianne, a week ago. We talked too much. That night I was tired and went to sleep, but she stayed up, sitting in hell on the sofa and weeping for my defunct love. This woke me up and I made a speech about how she was proposing once more to hide everything from R. then run away from him; or what? She said sorry, she proposed to confess to R., went confidently off, then three days later wrote a madly jealous letter saying she wanted to set out into the world.

Now and then I spend a bit of time at the Pinakothek.⁹ I've begun to get sick of Rubens orgies, all that flesh in the shop window. I've had too much of that myself, must move on to Titian. Here there's a subdued opulence, a sated golden glow, a combination of great strength and balmy peacefulness, together with the monumentality of Shakespeare. Yes, it would be a good idea to find somewhere and set up a yellow house, as Van Gogh suggests, in which to bring together people of ideas and character who would then be forced to see how they got on with one another. So social a business as the theatre can't be attacked from a number of single positions; what's needed is a reasonable consensus.

Friday 17th.
Eating cherries today in front of the mirror I saw my idiotic face. Those self-contained black bullets disappearing down my mouth made it look looser, more lascivious and contradictory than ever. It contains many elements of brutality, calm, slackness, boldness and cowardice, but as elements only, and it is more changeable and characterless than a landscape beneath scurrying clouds. That's why so many people find it impossible to retain ('you've too many of them' says Hedda).

⁹ Pinakothek. The Bavarian state art gallery, containing one of the great European collections.

In the evening I saw Granach in *From Morn to Midnight*[10] at the Neue Bühne. I observed that I'm starting to turn classic. Those extreme expenditures of effort in order to regurgitate certain themes (of a banal kind, or one that rapidly becomes banal) using any available means. People run down the classics for their services to form, and fail to see that it's the form that does the serving. Kaiser and co. with that journalistic (I'd term it) tendency to give every teeny-weeny feeling its own personalised, custom-built, uncompromising formulation only manage to isolate the feeling in question. Yes, smoothness of any kind puts me off, but perfection isn't smooth. We must get away from the grand gesture of tossing off an idea – of unfinishedness – and move on to tossing off a work of art, a fully realised idea – to the still grander gesture of 'finishedness plus'. Already beginning to crumble, to fade; evanescent, charmingly evasive, easily put together; not laboriously collected, sweated over, secured . . .

Kaiser, in so far as he works by means of a phenomenal emphasising of the word, certainly represents the last and most extreme effort to use words to achieve what the film achieves without them.

The Salvation Army scene is typical. The whole thing is grouped round one joke (whose effectiveness emanates from its victim). Having the penitents fall on the money as if they were starving is not a specially original idea, and if it is cheap one cannot blame Kaiser. But not every artist would have been content just to put forward the bare fact. He would have worked some art into it (even at the expense of external probability, thereby slowing things down, turning it all into an affair of words, a whole ghastly display of human sympathy with all its subtleties and gradations. Kaiser makes it a film shot.

Sunday 19th.

Things are beginning to pile up. Bi is coming to Nuremberg in July, this is my last week in Munich, and Marianne is coming. There will have to be a final escape, and it will be important not to get the wires crossed. What's more Aunt Marie[11] is sitting at home,

[10] *From Morn to Midnight*. Georg Kaiser's expressionist play, written in 1912 and first staged in 1917.

[11] Aunt Marie. Marie Zais, 1871–1939.

Father's sister from America, a lively, pleasant elderly lady, gentle and strong with good movements; I'm supposed to accompany her to Füssen tomorrow, but Father sees no point in the idea of looking in at Kimratshofen and has turned it down. One day he won't find it easy to reap what he is now sowing, I reckon. His lack of respect for his own blood makes me begin to lack respect for him. There are signs that the dénouement is approaching. The curtain is about to rise on the fourth Act . . .

End of June.
Marianne has been here for a week. It started badly, with her saying one night that R. had tried to rape her; she had been feeble. He had been in her, but she had acted so that he couldn't make it. There may have been some untruth in this, but I decided to write it off. We finished up at Possenhofen, where I got a wire from George summoning me. It was to do with Bi. By the time I arrived she had gone. This is a very hot summer.

JULY.

I'm as idle as a snake, time just slips by. I've been thinking about my *Summer Symphony*. Mar has been spending a week with me at Possenhofen. Marvellous. She is like the sea, always changing according to the light, even and strong. We ran through *Carmen*, *Rosenkavalier*. The nights have been as translucent as amber, I've slept like a hedgehog. The water washed us into the stiff green undergrowth, and watched as we joined our bodies. The shadows fled, I love her, she's more beautiful than ever: this has been the climax of the summer. The second part of the week was clouded. We went to China[12] with Heigei (she having met R. on Sunday and Monday and made another appointment with him for Thursday). Frank was healthy, cheerful, sweet-natured, he recognised me at once, he instantly fell for Otto who played at being a horse, devoured hats with his boot-sole and so forth. He reacted less to Marianne, perhaps because she doesn't love him enough; and then when he doesn't go to her she gets colder. All the same, she's very sweet to him, it would be marvellous if she were to bring him up. Incidentally she came on a note of mine referring in frivolous terms to R.'s assault, and began accusing me of lying. She's as jealous as a negress, and tyrants seldom get told the truth. I'm too lazy for childish disputes and too Asiatic to wish to die for Truth at the stake. And she has started sprawling around all my affairs and spying where she can and trying to put me against Bi and my friends. I love her, but she's not clever. And sooner or later she's going to make me rebel. Admittedly, it's only the bad things that I note in this book, and her sweetness and the grace that informs every single breath she draws, her strong resonance and a lot else is not to be found here.

For a long time I idled. After that Cas and I wrote a big film in three days, lots of pages, a hundred and fifty shots, dripping with sweat and stinking like goats below table level. It's called *Drei im Turm*[13] and is for Marianne.

I've been swimming, drinking lemonade, reading detective

---

[12] China. Presumably Kimratshofen.
[13] Three in a Tower. In *Texte für Filme I*.

stories and writing one of my own called *Javameier*.[14] Being an engineer is good fun.

On Frank's third birthday I went to see Bi at Utting.[15] She was easy and good, we bathed, sat under the trees; but Frank has almost vanished from her mind, she didn't write for his birthday till today and takes no steps to see him. I must work twice as hard so that I can have him with me.

[14] Meier from Java. In vol. 11 of the collected German edition of 1967, p. 62. Meier is an engineer.

[15] Utting. On the West shore of the Ammer-See, some thirty miles south of Augsburg.

AUGUST.

Saturday 13th.
The night's not over, and it's raining and the wind is still blowing.
I got up, we couldn't sleep, neither Marianne nor I, I'm in my
dressing-gown sitting on the sofa with my arms and legs shaking,
it's an attack of loneliness.

Mar has been here for ages, we sat at the same table, sleep in the
same bed and quarrel if we aren't also thinking the same thought.
She is lovely and good, very multifarious; just that the room is too
constricted and myself perhaps likewise ... I'm doing nothing,
thinking nothing, experiencing nothing.

Tuesday 16th.
She left for Wiesbaden early this morning. She has broken with R.
for good, so no apartment there, and not much money...

Wednesday 17th.
I can still see her face as the train moved off: pale under its brown,
light, like a blossom, smiling. The hunt for her is on once more.

Thursday 25th.
Divided between fresh film schemes and Sinclair's *Metropolis*:[16]
observe the results of 'work for its own sake'. Did those bourgeois
need a pretext, did work have to be sanctified? Suddenly it became
a duty. Chucked into Tahiti, a means of getting away from itself.
Work in order to be able to stop working. And then entertainment,
sport, pastime. Then test, means to power, self-respect.

Saturday 27th.
I've been wrestling with the resources of poetry. The stage can
build up towards its 'outbursts' and as a result can let its language
be purely ornamental, flowerlike and brutal, a cold garment.
What's interesting and what's poetic are different in kind. The
colour of a scene has little to do with its tension. Looking at the
offspring you can't tell if the muse was seductive or not. Food is
still the motive force...

[16] *The Metropolis* by Upton Sinclair was published in English in 1908.

Monday 29th.

I've written the 'Ballad of the Love-Death',[17] which signifies a relaxation of my language and a step towards the middle. Let yourself get involved with language, and it soon becomes like chewing india-rubber. Cynicism however blasts rocks open.

Orge is against any kind of restriction. He can't stand working with his hands tied – digging out a particular story. He refuses to rape people in order to make a point.

[17] 'Ballad of the Love-Death'. *Poems 1913–1956*, p. 71.

SEPTEMBER

Friday [2nd].
They've pulled out my front tooth, smashed up half my jaw. I put
on my hard hat while Orge and Hei dragged me off to Hei's. There
we sang 'Asleep on the Deep'[18] and 'The Red Sarafan',[19] and Hei
read from the tale of Apollonius of Tyre.[20] Orge played the piano
like a pig – the Maiden's Prayer and Radetsky [March] – and
laughed till his teeth wobbled. I lay in the arm chair feeling ill. I'm
continually sad and empty.

Sunday [4th].
Wondering what Kipling had done for the nation that 'civilised'
our world I made the epoch-making discovery that nobody has yet
described the big city as a jungle. Where are its heroes, its
colonisers, its victims? The hostility of the big city, its malignant
stony consistency, its babylonian confusion of language – in short
its poetry has not yet been created.

Tuesday [6th].
Whatever happens it's a mistake to get too far away from simple
objectives. Ever since a couple of fellows first put cheap planks
across some brandy casks and began conducting some sort of trade
in public, the entertainment of the spectator was the objective
people paid for. Those gaping brewers, coopers, tax farmers
would habitually rest there, and shortly afterwards would satisfy
their subterranean but thoroughly terrestrial instincts in the
cheapest possible way, likewise their celestial ones, thereby
creating a substitute for any dangerous excesses right in the centre
of the perimeter of their well-protected abdominal stockade. Soon
the simple adventures had to be salted with sophisticated practical
maxims, rendered more digestible by gently insidious atmos-
pherics, spiced with semi-concealed or impertinently explosive
jokes. Now the evolution has reached its end with nothing but the

---

[18] 'Asleep on the Deep'. English equivalent of 'Der Seemannslos', a favourite
nineteenth century song often cited by Brecht.
[19] 'The Red Sarafan'. Russian folksong.
[20] Apollonius of Tyre. Story derived from a Greek original, existing in many
languages and versions.

vanity of the actors satisfying that of an auditorium full of cooks and gastronomic hangers-on.

Thursday 15th.

I've got nothing to do, am sleeping badly, losing weight. On my chaise-longue I've been sporadically reading Charles-Louis Philippe and enjoying him.[21] *Marie Donadieu* and *Bubu* are the best ones. In addition I've been reading Karl Kraus. Have hardly had any letters. What's Bi up to? The migrating birds shit on me and my island. But nothing grows there. I'm more or less mulling over a business called *Freedom* or *The Antagonists*.[22] It's a play of conflict, East-West, with an underground issue: scene, the back of beyond. It needs the large-scale forms of *Baal*. But the summer has virtually demolished me. I now (and only now) know what a woman is, and I know about bed love and a lot else, but I've shed my impertinence, my incredible naivety, naive incredulousness, the security of not knowing. All the same things are at any rate getting quieter, I can see wider ramifications even if I don't feel strong enough. My fingers are furry, my hands are all thumbs; and then this distrust of all that has come down to us ... Yet experiments are uncongenial to me. Nature makes no experiments. Nothing that's alive is ever petty, nor is there such a thing as art without detachment. People who are up in the clouds lose too much by evaporation. Moreover it's important not to display one's insides but always to remain dark and bulky. No showing off, that's it.

Friday 16th.

I've spent the whole day working on my play *Back of Beyond* or *The Forest* or *Jungle* or *The Antagonists* or *George Garga*.[23] I started out by writing the marginal scene called 'Green papered attic'. It's now passable so far as the language goes. Currently I'm writing on quite small thin sheets of paper, walking under the trees; not one word in an enclosed space. The weather is good, I walk for hours to the sound of falling chestnuts all round me. At the same time, I'm proceeding absolutely relaxedly, not committing myself too soon.

[21] Philippe. French novelist, author of *Bubu de Montparnasse* etc.

[22] This and the following entry represent the first germs of *In the Jungle of Cities*, Brecht's third play.

[23] George Garga. Principal character in *In the Jungle of Cities*.

It was only when half-way through the first scene that I got a complete picture of G. Garga. Much later I constructed the framework of the plot, which I've put virtually no weight on. Everything's fluid, I love approximation. In among this I sketch sentences from all the various scenes together with individual entrances. It's all growing, almost of its own accord, and heading towards the mid-point, as though I were writing from memory.

I'm in good form, taking no interest in things, neglecting clothes, meals, company, and feeling calm and stable as I write. Each word has broken out of its shell; sentences come thrusting up straight from my breast. I just copy them down.

Sunday 18th.
I've been working non-stop. Finished the first scene yesterday, also parts of others. The second today, then half the third this evening, preceded by the last. Every word out of doors. Spent two hours by the Lech today in a cold wind, and I noticed it too late.

Monday 19th.
Worked down by the Lech for three or four hours this morning. Afterwards I had a bit of a temperature, a swimming head. Tomorrow's the two law-suits,[24] and I'm due to appear. It upsets me having to stop work.

> Louis Philippe[25]
> Soyka[26]
> Armstrong film[27]
> Titian
> *Turm* film
> Ballad of the Love-Death.
> George Garga or The Jungle.
> Marianne by the lake.

Soyons amis, Cinna![28]

---

[24] Law-suits. See note on 'my case' p. 83.
[25] Louis Philippe. The author, not the king.
[26] Otto Soyka, 1882–1955, Austrian writer of psychological adventure stories.
[27] Billy Armstrong, actor in Mack Sennett's films.
[28] 'Soyons amis'. Quotation from Corneille's *Cinna*, V, 3.

End of September 1921 to mid-February 1922.

SEPTEMBER

27th.

I've been reading Feuerbach's[1] account of the murders committed by a priest, a dignified and well-read man who had the energy and the knowledge of people to work his way up despite innately evil urges to the position of rector and estate owner, and had a strong sense of morality, being anxious at the same time to remain on good terms with God. This is interesting for its bearing on the story of God. The man was an exemplary citizen. He impregnated three women of the people, lived with them for a considerable time, set great store by their loyalty, earned their love and looked after the children. In order to safeguard public morality, likewise to preserve his own honour and the respect of his fellow-citizens, he polished off one of these girls by quietly murdering her. She proved no burden to his conscience. He was capable of trampling on the body with his feet in order to push it into the ground (for her hands were rigidly fixed in a gesture of supplication, so you tripped over them when threshing the corn). The murdered woman had a green linen unbrella which he carried for many years; he seemed to deserve his acquired possession. In prison he smilingly denied everything for the first four years and defended himself like a man. Then in a kind of nervous breakdown he confessed. From the official records it appears that just before confessing he was looking out of the window and saw a murderer going to his death. The man's cheerfulness and poise amazed him, all the more so in the case of a man who 'moreover was merely a Jew'. Thereafter he ate little, heard 'a spine-chillingly funereal drum' following the Angelus, and shortly after that confessed. He asked them to take into consideration in his favour the fact that he had done everything he could to avoid a public scandal.

28th.

I doubt if there is any greater immorality a dramatist can display than a certain complacency about that weakness of the human race which consists in being born with a herd instinct but lacking the

---

[1] Feuerbach. Brecht refers to the 'Franz Riembauer' episode in P. J. A. von Feuerbach's *Aktenmässige Darstellung merkwürdiger Verbrechen* (Some Strange Crimes As Portrayed In The Documents), 1808–11.

qualities which the formation of a herd calls for. Nearly every bourgeois institution, practically our entire morality, virtually the whole Christian legend, are based on man's fear of being alone, thus distracting his attention from his total abandonment on this planet, his infinitesimal significance and barely perceptible roots. Almost any conceivable tragedy situated within the framework of the family, together with all the crimes involved therein, can be justified (dramatically exploited) by its consolidation of the family as an institution, in that it accepts the latter's possibility as pre-ordained and concentrates entirely on the martyrdoms which it entails. Any dramatist attempting to raise the question of its pre-ordination had better look out, however. He is a crow feeding on crow's eyes. Qui mange du pape en meurt.

Take Joseph Galgei and the few ideas that penetrate his thick skull. He has no relationship with his fate, human communication could hardly be bothered with him, no deal could be done with him, he was merely dealt in. What attracted him was the difficulty and complication of committing an injustice. They steer a murder in his way and thereafter he conducts himself like a murderer, rather subdued, rather drunk, rather pleased with himself and very much at the end of his tether. But above all like someone who cannot grasp the real situation. Whether he did (the fact that he didn't) commit the murder is a matter of indifference.

29th.

Like any other artist the imaginative writer too should be able to work from the female body. Not by portraying it but by recreating its measurements in all the proportions of his work. The body's outlines become those of his composition; just as our sight of the former heightens our sense of life, so must our appreciation of the latter.

I plod along under the chestnut trees, whistle up the Holy Ghost, read detective stories over my coffee and cannot get moving. I'm walking round in a circle, keeping the maypole on my right all the time, I'm wearing out my boots. I'm getting so melancholeric. Yes, of course the style (G. Garga's) has got to be dry and matter-of-fact, of course the momentum has to rip through every scene, of course the whole thing has to be as serious as playing can ever be. The Malay is as impervious to attack as any suicide, so that he virtually has to invent his own ethic in order to be able to perish by it. In the end there are strikes against him, which is no kind of a dramatic device. ('I shall trample down my fields and fart the whole ammunition dump into the dawn air. I'll abandon him to nausea, to self-centredness, to boredom. He shall be devoured by nothingness.')

30th
Walter rushes into the Kraal.

'The evidence is now conclusive. Downstairs in the cupboard the schnaps bottle's suffering from consumption. Up here there's a cupboard with a mug been sitting in it for months on end, and what's that mug got in it? Schnaps . . .'[2]

'It's a libel. You're the boozer. I smelt it on your breath, you only smelt it from my cupboard. You're dragging in an innocent man. A lousy thing to do! Infamous!'

'Are you telling me it's the old schnaps?'

'Yes, I'm not like you. I don't stash it in my stomach half consumed, but unconsumed – in my mug.'

'When you've been getting so little?'

'Are you suggesting my abstemiousness will be the death of me? I'd sooner be taken to the crematorium any day.'

What sabotages the drama is the dishonesty of its means – its 'moyens' as George calls them. If I want to portray a struggle, it will probably be one between two people, not between two systems. This conditions all the characters' outer curves; the struggle has to be portrayed by them. The fate of the characters remains a matter of taste. The extent to which the individuals become aware of their curves, then resist them, is what produces the personal climate, in other words the poetic element. Acts of resistance create the cosmic aspect. Each of the protagonists in the struggle has to be given every possible opportunity, but one mustn't set out to prove anything.

Tonight, conversation with George about the Gent.[3] The Gent obtrudes himself on our attention simply by being unobtrusive.

---

[2] Mug. The German has 'Tasche', but this appears to be a likely misreading for 'Tasse'.

[3] Gent. Brecht uses the English term.

He manages to remain anonymous and incognito. He never profanes anything. He is colourless, a kind of water-colour wash that has been wiped away with a sponge. He may say clever things so long as there's no risk, so that you remember them without remembering who said them. He is matter-of-fact; what he regards as a fact is not the subject of a conversation but the conversation itself. The Gent is never ironical but always serious, concentrating on the fact of the matter. He pays exactly as much attention to people as the conversation warrants. The Gent will defend anything under the sun for the sake of conversation, but without obstinacy and only if it can be done without a fuss. If he is slightly perverse, moreover, he will actually defend the things he minds about. Though he may not be all that satisfactory to talk to, he is an admirable person to live with.

OCTOBER.

1st.

I've been revising the second scene. It's a hell of a job in the open air. But the relationships are becoming simpler and more human all the same. Though the struggle may be becoming over-intellectual. I must stir in some more ingredients, more haggling over coffee, forenoon, belches, primitive life ... At the same time I'm beginning to feel an urge to write plays about stupid people. 'Mankind in Pursuit of Money', that kind of thing, fleeting, colourful, malicious plays, a wild life with Kaffirs and caryatids, a fast-moving plot.

2nd.

Man is the diadem of creation, he can do anything. He can turn one of Eden's apples into shit. Look at the Merchant: a pallid tableau, crass immorality, piled on. Shakespeare's not like that. Nothing that's alive is immoral. A funeral speech is, though, for a start. Here we have the story of an immoral contract. A man is more than a contract, than ships or money or happiness. He's not been thought out; he's operative. Here is a (battered, violated, spat-upon) fellow who wants to break some damned neck with the help of the law, and what the law does is to help dislocate his wrists for him. It is a father whose only daughter has been stolen. He is not particularly nice. (No use is made of this, it would undermine the ground we're standing on.) Generally speaking the story is strong enough to support all kinds of luxuries. It's precisely people who act in precisely this way. Not like later, when the remarkable thing becomes the fact that this kind of people act like this. People in those days were still sufficiently interested in the plot. Today the same need is catered for by the novel. One need is satisfied by this play; the need for justice. The man knows we have invested something in it. We shan't look this horse in the mouth. We enjoy demolishing. The pretext: he's so immoral. In the old days people believed so as not to spoil the fun. Now their only fun is not believing. So one has to offer them things they can not believe in. And since the swindle now operates primarily in the realm of ideals, that's where their plays are located.

It's Sunday, the Lord's Day. I've got a better skin on, am

wearing yellow leather tubes, have a hard hat on top of me. We stroll up the yellow autumnal alley, two couples of us. On the Lord's Day they don't remove the tree corpses. The girl I'm walking with is a pale, heavily powdered pianist who is forced to cook at home and cultivates *odium vitae*, saying 'Dying is painful. But sooner dead than alive'. And at the same time is good white flesh; tolerant. Hei, elegant, hardboiled, conceited and really on top of things (being on solid ground), walking with her sister, wholly uninteresting, stupid, thick-legged. A little blue-(silk)stocking. Hei looking like a crusader beside her, unawares, unrelated, full of schnaps at night, in the armchair, if he gets her he'll be first of the primitives, communication via the flesh, as it turned out he went in front, I behind, it was the Lord's Day, he had money for schnaps. The only non-accident: that the body opened. Orge and I whistled duets to the guitar, he rummaged about in the chinashop a bit, Hei sat in his chair creating silence, I felt for a hand which proved to be soft, rather boneless and yielded only to be dropped. I sang to the guitar though my f's were wretched, being difficult to bring out without teeth.

Enter, hand on her heart, the Jewess of Berlin. For the last six months, she says, there's been a youth courting her, but she feels tied; I can't untie her. She encloses a certificate from a woman friend, reckoning up our good and bad features. It's full of bad advice. All the same, the despair of these limited liability lovers gets on my nerves. I write her a matter-of-fact letter. Earlier, when in a mess, I had written her a good letter – it was a quiet moment, I was clear-headed – saying 'you need good underwear', an act of brutality, a piece of erotic opportunism? There has been no answer. Peccavi.

3rd.
'Perversion is nothing but the morbid intensification of a normal desire.' Jam for the playhouse! They sell posters here. And for the truffle-hounds there are perversions of the innermost feelings, holy perversions. What's more, St. Anthony is a product of pathology, though this does nothing to explain him, darlings. The only point of pathology is to help you see, since you've such weak eyesight, specially when up against a mirror. All the same mankind is a lot healthier than tapeworms and priests might think. It is healthy

enough to have invented tragedy and algolagnia.[4] The pathological element is the true hero. First on account of its vitality and secondly because it stands out head and shoulders (or possibly a phallus's length) above the crowd. Speaking for myself, a decently made play demands a smoothly functioning digestion. Which should even tackle stones. That's to say the air must be clear. The washing-up must have been done. The heavens mustn't spring any leaks. But must remain clean, hard and impervious to attack. That fat beast mankind has patience, and to spare. And this planet has its ice ages.

'True, their skins are thick.[5] All they do is scrape away their leprosy. Put a shot into them, and water runs out. Snot. Yet there's more inside. Disasters happen intermittently. There are whirlpools for the thick-skinned. Every now and then one of them is found strangled. For which air alone was responsible.'

'I shall kick my boots in your face. They're not interested in your face. Ruffian! You're putting me off, and time is trickling away. "Waters can take on entire mountains," I know. You're working yourself up to attack me. Between hedgehog and hedgehog there can be nothing but conflict. But watch out: sometimes I deceive people about what I want. They let me have it, then find they are on slippery ground.' (Garga to Shlink.)

'True, I love dry knowledge, I would be like the leathern Pandects.[6] Like the engineers of those green water-conduits, trickling like snot over the stones, only to be dammed up and used to drive paper-mills. I've more important business here than to wreck my boots trampling on you. Asia is still there for the asking, and I shall buy it up with the fanatical dryness of a scientist.'

'There's nothing you can do in Asia. It's here you must fight your battles, with the wooden rafters for your sky. Fail against just one man, and you won't need to leave the room. You can't combat Kismet with all the tobacco fields in Virginia. Your expansionist mania has tripped over a little corpse that was purring away and took no interest in you.'

[4] Algolagnia. Term for Masochism introduced into German by the Munich psychiatrist Schrenck-Notzing and into English by Havelock Ellis.

[5] The quotations in this entry are experiments in the heightened dialogue style of *In the Jungle of Cities*, based on that of Rimbaud's 'Une Saison en Enfer'.

[6] Pandects. Justinian's *Digesta* of Roman law.

Already half-rejected by Cassirer, my bundle of manuscripts has now been returned by Kiepenheuer with polite thanks. Very encouraging for me. It's a bad situation. Well, I don't need to make a living out of it. It would be beneath me to strain myself.

4th

I've been wallowing in the Rimbaud volume, borrowing a passage here and there. How the whole thing glows! Phosphorescent paper! And his shoulders are solid bronze ... Whenever I'm working and the lava has begun to flow, I see the West gloomily burning and believe in its vitality.

Büchner's *Danton* at the municipal theatre. A superb melodrama. Without Shakespeare's roundedness, edgier, more intellectualised, more fragmentary, an ecstatic sequence of scenes, philosophically a panorama. This kind of thing is no longer a model, more a powerful aid.

'That parchment-bound devil is haunting us still. You are all mistaken. He has wrapped his club foot in paper, and is dropping a strong poison in our gristly ears. Each time he turns up the view deepens at the ultraviolet end of the spectrum; the place becomes a naked island.'

I've been spending a lot of time with Orge. He goes around with those acute ears of his, visits his study conscientiously and keeps talking about the concept of Imagination. At the same time he wants to get married. He fancies he knows what a woman is. Has never had one. But wants to live with one in a little hut. He thinks he's cheating the devil out of his percentage. The devil is putting it on the bill. What a child he is. He keeps saying 'Well, a woman naturally had to realise that ...' etc. A woman has no imagination (hence no sense of humour either), she doesn't need any, she's got her love even if it sometimes lacks understanding. He remarks, in a deliberately light tone designed to brush the ghosts away, 'She'll sit in a corner of the room spinning, and look at her man'. (He only needs to be there!) I don't know if he realises that 'a' woman leads no kind of intellectual life; certainly he doesn't realise that it takes an intellectual being to permit freedom and grant a certain distance. He is twenty-eight. He is innocent.

5th

It seems essential to make Garga a genius. Otherwise he'll just be a prizefighter. He mustn't merely fight, but should smoke, behave childishly, get interested. That can't depend on his power of expression alone. It's a matter of his actions. A certain superiority, a childlike cynicism, a kind of nonchalance ... He should walk slowly: lazy, revolutionary, brutal, with large limbs. The great dialogue passages are wholly metaphysical, their corporality and full-bloodedness result from the passion with which the fight in question is waged. Nor am I creating visages so much as visions. This is where Expressionism comes in. Not powers in human form, but humans as spiritual beings. My starting point really is the concept of a story. This and the people are what I begin with. I create the story, or rather it creates me.

That black addiction of the brain: winning.

6th

Yes, there was something petty about the Hauptmann era.[7] Its not very intelligent accuracy in the portrayal of people, its confidence that the material would do the trick left to itself, its mingling of passion and hysteria. In earlier times this nation had more imagination perhaps. Pettiness triumphed by means of decoration, there was enough ornament to ensure that. As for that unbridled pedant J. Paul, his philistine qualities were overridden by an irresistible discursiveness and wealth of elaboration. Today, when the structure is clearly that of the iron age, a talent like Hauptmann's, comparable as it is to that of Keller, Storm and Raabe, is no longer a source of strength.

7th

Autumn is now fully upon us. Today I drank a strong light beer, grew unsteady on my pins, skidded up the walk beneath the trees. The leaves were brown, thin, paper-dry, with the new moon coolly overhead. Yellow and brown. There's an October Fair now on: beer booths, clowns, actors, a band. You ride on roundabouts that sling you into the air. You swing, powered by your own muscles. How boring it all is. What lavatory-tile faces! What

---

[7] The German authors referred to in this entry are Gerhart Hauptmann, 1862–1946, the playwright; Jean Paul Richter, 1763–1825, the novelist; Gottfried Keller, 1819–90, Swiss novelist and story writer; Theodor Storm, 1817–88, story writer and poet; and Wilhelm Raabe, 1831–1910, novelist.

voices, like domestic animals! The sideshows add to the
romanticism; the people, dumb, sinful and patient, lets itself be
titillated. One can't live for ever.

8th

There aren't all that many people who are so prolific they can let
their arse be licked without getting submerged in Bohemia.
Success is a great antidote to the bohemian life, aside from those
cases where a fellow's chest is puffed out with adoration of his own
work. You have to be very strong to have any hope of winning the
fight against corrosion.

9th

'To the cuckolded lover too far away'. Hedda, writing from Berlin
asks 'If you're coming to Berlin to see me shall I get you a room?
As your wife? If so I have been breaking my marriage vows for the
past few months'. There follow arguments: a tooth for a tooth, a
horn for a horn. I should give her her freedom. It's the only way I
can now help her. – I find all the talk depressing, and the evidence
of cowardice; but am content with the solution. Have asked her to
get me a room.

   This evening I had a bit of a head after drinking beer and going
to the café. That is, I was rather restless, my hands actually shook, I
could only write with reluctance yet didn't want to go to bed. On
top of that it has been four days since I had any letters. So I opened
my drawer, and there, among a disorderly heap of other papers, lay
He's letter,[8] slightly crumped, almost as if it had been screwed into
a ball: a yellow sheet of paper, a yellow, creased, exceedingly,
extremely eye-catching yellow paper corpse, covered in hasty
handwriting with strong up-strokes in a rather watery ink, all
neatly laid out, summarily phrased and not lacking in vanity. I
don't know what it was that so fascinated me about this; I've no
feelings that need to be suppressed, I'm not in love this time, and
yet once again it's as though I could taste the tears running down a
face, and touch shoulders that shake with weeping, and hear the
many words, bitter and imploring, ever so carefully prepared, so

---

[8] He's letter. See the resulting poem 'An inscription touches off sentimental
memories' in *Poems 1913–1956*, p. 85.

helplessly floundering, along with the actions that have now, weeks later, come to seem unworthy, now that there is something new to be lived through with virtually no transition but once again with love and not without pangs of conscience; and the whole thing's so ridiculous, the past martyrdom, the feeling now replaced by other feelings, the smooth transition, repression, auctioning off the remains. Today the woman closest to my heart speaks Malay. Water has flowed from my eyes and they have started gazing at a new fetish. How simple it all is, how smoothly it goes, how the body's dark urges will make it recognise the right way and a spasm will remain a spasm, once it's over . . .

10th

True enough, where those related to me are concerned I can be cold and cynical. I drag a lot of things in the dirt, and I make a great many demands. Now and then however I have simply grown sad, not angry or contemptuous or vindictive. Today a girl treated me impolitely who had loved me some years back. She said she wanted to take a photograph, and she kept me waiting. Her feelings are a matter of indifference to me, but I was depressed by her impoliteness, as though it meant something.

11th

There are moments when I think how simple it would be if we all had the same problems. We would surely be able to say 'All women are faithless, all men are corruptible' if it weren't for the fact that a lot of women are cold and a lot of men cowardly or stupid about money.

12th

Some evenings we drink lots of beer, go on the swing-boats and gossip like old women. I can't do much work. *Jungle*'s action has ground to a halt; it's too full of literature. The idle chatter of a couple of littérateurs.

1

Moon swung bald in the violet
Sky above the silk mill's stack.
Meanwhile I, God's bare-arsed varlet
Soaped the cord inside the sack.

2
Through the absinthe night I blundered –
I, whose feelings could be smelt
Half-felt feelings barely plundered
As if from a butcher's shelf.

3
Did you never wring your hands then
In an alcoholic fog
Bald, in those green half-lights standing
Swaying between wolf and dog?

4
Did you feel no short celestial
Singing as you swapped your drink –
Did you, terrified and bestial
Swill an 'Ave!' down the sink?

5
If, submerged in bitter feeling
I dredge up a childish song
Even if it's blotched and peeling
With a verse or two that long ...

6
Floats across the stagnant yellow
Puddles of depravity:
Then my skin turns cold, dear fellow
Like snow biting into me.

7
As the sky begins to lower
To my ravaged heart I cling
Tenderly. Then I blew over
Like a snowstorm in the spring.⁹

13th
Over coffee and elevenses I leafed through Str[indberg]'s fat novel,
a work by that great genius for the defence, that campaigner for

⁹ First version of the poem called 'März' (March) in vol. 8 of the German
collected works, 1967, p. 104.

men's rights, which contains such incomparable chapters as the
burial episode in *The Red Room*[10] and the death of the writer Axel
E. in the *Gothic Stories*. But what domestic details, and doesn't he
go on washing his underwear! Look out when he gets down to the
proofs! A theologian of Heaven-via-Bed . . . Such barbarities! The
cuckold founding a club and inviting humanity to join it. Yet look
at his concreteness: potted newspaper, complete with magazine
section, political comment and small ads.

14th

Slowly my play *Jungle* has been making headway. During those
autumn nights with their penetrating white mists. It has been
growing unevenly, in something of a muddle. But I'm anxious not
to fall for an idea. And the scenes should be performed quite
lightly, on a makeshift stage against a background of pasteboard
and watercolour, lightly knocked together.

15th

It's half past one. But I don't at all want to go to bed. I'd sooner be
bored. How little time we have, and to think that we kill it . . .

I took a trip to Nuremberg. It was Sunday, so Bi and I spent the
afternoon in the cinema and the evening at a café. They detained us
because I sent a cup of coffee back. Bi was splendid. She sat quite
unaffected among a crowd of people all of whom were instinctively
hating me, and she felt this. My train left at half past one. I
wandered around the castle in the cold night, smoked, drank
schnaps. Then I boarded the train and hunched there eating,
sleeping, cursing, dreaming, smoking and boozing for ten hours.
By the time we were nearing Höchst I was in a sweat; it's occupied
territory there, and I had my revolver with me. In Frankfurt I
bought a cigar box, but the post office was shut and the train had
no ornate WC to hide it in. However, no check. At M[arianne]'s I
felt immediately at home.

24th

This is a tarts' town.[11] Powder, flesh, sensation. Slick pavements,
dead straight streets. Chemise-y faces. Frenchmen with nigger

[10] Strindberg's first novel, *The Red Room*, appeared in Swedish in 1878.
[11] A tarts' town. Wiesbaden, then under French occupation.

bands, dogs, cocottes. Brightly lit cafés, amazing prices, unpleasant looking people, a city with all its goods in the shop window ... It's just as boring here.

25th

I'm staying in the Moritzstrasse, slept till nine (part of the time in a hard bed), with Marianne till eleven in the spotlessly clean little room, escorted her to the theatre, then went for a walk. Smoked, drank, gossipped. From one till six. Saw *Butterfly* in rubbishy sets, atrociously directed, which led me to infer that from the Vltava to the Tiber the yokels are making money, yet not a soul in these flatlands has any idea how to serve a slap-up supper. M. gave a really rather bad performance as the lady, in conformity with the level of the whole affair. Her innate magnificence back home has now evaporated. A theatre for niggers... The next day, being on my own, I mapped out a play called *Joan*,[12] complete with scenario, list of characters and intellectual props. It's as though I had left M. the previous evening, dreamt about her and again run into her early this morning. Living with her is good and never bores one. That isn't simply because I love her. Why am I incapable of writing about people I love? One only sees objective facts; feelings are too strong. She's clever and has an instinctive sense of life. Got no use for theories. She is utterly human. R. was here for one day, there was a moment when she was planning to get rid of him, but then she discussed the most intimate things with him, but without letting him get near her. She won't accept any more money, saying he can use it to gamble on the stock exchange; then goes off with him to buy a fur jacket for several thousand marks and looks marvellous in it. He has such good taste ... But she has borrowed the money for it. And everything she does is right, it's not bad, you can't draw any conclusions about her from it, she's merely living among other people and with them, tackling difficulties without getting obsessed and taking things easy without making herself cheap. Certainly she is on the right road, her walk along it may be a bit less certain, she has the odd pang of conscience and I know more than she does, but it's a good battle and you can count on her, and quite apart from that I love her and can't bother myself about

[12] Scraps of Brecht's planned Pope Joan play have survived.

what can't be changed. In other words I'm not going to alter her like an idiot but shall wait for her to be altered by love; and all the time she's becoming more like she used to be in the good days, before R. and the theatre.

26th

Now that I have established the plan of those incidents that took place in Rome in the year 860, as specified by my iron will, a certain childish curiosity, along with a desire to get my hooks on words, errors, matters of fact, led me to hunt up the available literature about Joan. There isn't any. Those country bumpkins and plagiarists who batten on the tolerance of grown up elementary school kids, those impotent source-mongers who are acquainted with everything and know nothing, who write political history five hundred times over from five different points of view without ever communicating a picture of the period that might let you see, for instance, what the Pope ate and drank, how he loved and was served, how he got dressed, whether he washed himself and how often, and how he felt about smoking ... And not one single account of the fashions, crafts, business transactions, or the social situation of merchants, soldiers, priests. There were no novels to help out, and history with its umpteen fat volumes comes nowhere near supplying as much of the essence of public life as one gets from one solitary newspaper. Look where you will, you find nothing, nothing but ideological think-pieces and miserable attempts to insinuate a meaning into the whole external calendar of European public sensations. (One day when I've the time I'd like to write an account of the events and conduct of a single year in the life of a German city. In the style of [Tacitus'] *Germania*. I only know of one decent travel writer, an American journalist called [the name has been left blank], a 'shallow chatterbox' with a practical mind.

27th

Marianne and I had an argument about taste. She stood up for tarts' taste, which I wrote off as a matter of talent, of Intimate Theatre taste. Most of the time what tarts are clothing is their physique, not their bodies. They stylise their face till it looks like a flowershop, it looks as if they had pulled it on like a glove, they smell of perfumed sweat, they aren't visions so much as displays, painted stone, statuettes in cardboard boxes. The trees in the background look naked, crude, tasteless. Instead of this clothes ought to look improvised and amateurish, a bit relaxed yet still orderly, and mainly so out of politeness. One shouldn't see the clothers but the woman. The woman isn't even the picture designed for this frame; in fact the picture is painted on air. How crude they are, these shifting illustrations to the text 'Today thou shalt be with Me in Paradise'. Tarts' clothes are professional clichés, draperies without imagination or humour, something clear and tangible; it's as though a dress had an independent life – a lovely dress rather than the dress of a lovely woman (though that doesn't mean that I don't want, indeed insist, that her loveliness should be heightened by the dress, but it has to be a cheat, a trick, a knack, the dress has to be so self-denying that after doing most of the work it retreats unapplauded into the background, with a modest smile . . .).

One loves a Frenchwoman of that sort much as one smokes a cigarette when surrounded by connoisseurs: one smokes it, but not right to the end. As it goes on dwindling away, transforming itself into smoke, one chucks it away; but the smell hangs around one's clothes for ages. (Longer than around one's mouth.) The trouble is, though, that this is such a stale analogy.

28th

I sat through *Rheingold*, a dreadfully decrepit performance. The orchestra has softening of the bones, the whole thing's flat-footed. The godlings do their ranting amid carefully executed imitations of Jurassic rock formations, while as for the clouds of steam coming up from the wash-house where they scrub Wotan's dirty underclothes, they are enough to make you sick. Amazing how Marianne's lovely delicate voice stands out.

29th

Then I saw a little one-acter of Charlie Chaplin's.[13] It's called *The Face on the Bar-Room Floor* and is the most profoundly moving

---

[13] It was not till 1921 that the Germans were able to import Chaplin's films. In 1944 Brecht wrote a poem (*Poems 1913–1956* p. 393) about this film, whose German title was 'Alkohol und Liebe'.

thing I've ever seen in the cinema: utterly simple. It's about a painter who enters a bar, has a drink and 'because you folk have been so good to me' narrates the story of his own downfall, which is that of a girl who has gone off with a bloated plutocrat. He sees her again, drunk and in rags, and it's 'the profanation of his ideal', she's fat and has children, at which he puts his hat on askew and goes off upstage into the darkness, staggering as if he had been hit on the head, all askew, my God, all askew as if he'd been blown off course by the wind, all windblown like no one you ever saw. And then the teller of the story gets drunker and drunker, and his need to communicate ever stronger and more painful, so he asks for 'a bit of that chalk you put on the tips of your billiard cues' and draws the loved one's portrait on the floor – only to produce a series of circles. He slithers around on it, quarrels with all and sundry, gets chucked out and goes on drawing on the pavement – more circles – and gets chucked back in and goes on drawing there and chucks them all out and they pop their heads in at the windows and he's drawing on the floor and the end of the whole thing is: suddenly, just as he was trying to add a particularly artistic curl to the loved one's hair, he let out a dreadful shriek and collapsed on top of his picture, dead ... drunk ... (ivre ... mort ...). Chaplin's face is always impassive, as though waxed over, a single expressive twitch rips it apart, very simple, strong, worried. A pallid clown's face complete with thick moustache, long artist's hair and a clown's tricks: he messes up his coat, sits on his palette, gives an agonised lurch, tackles a portrait by – of all things – elaborating the backside. But nothing could be more profoundly moving, it's unadulterated art. Children and grown-ups laugh at the poor man, and he knows it: this nonstop laughter in the auditorium is an integral part of the film, which is itself deadly earnest and of a quite alarming objectivity and sadness. The film owes (part of) its effectiveness to the brutality of its audience.

30th

Such fear of cold Chicago ...

Those women suddenly waking up to the fact that they may one day have to wash their silk blouses, or it might snow on their grand dresses and they'll be left merely with the warmth of the public establishments and the light of the gas lanterns. That's where all the bad instincts originate, the low habits, the play-acting. And those men suddenly becoming aware of their responsibilities or of the indifference of those public places, the idiotic and destructive significance of printed paper, one's utter abandonment to infinitesimal differences of calculation, payment, luck, the way a strong, complex and costly organism can be demolished by some barely measurable change in the atmosphere, a trick of the wind, sacrificed without either sacrificer or god.

31st

The question is whether it isn't possible to break the gloomy law of causal necessity within Man . . . Inexorably our actions bring about some alteration in our environment and our inner selves. Is there no grace, no credit, is there no one who does *not* believe in our sins, who thinks better of us than we ourselves do; why don't they stop adapting themselves to us, why do they have to be so poverty-stricken, so bare and beggarly as to wear their purple only in the light, and why can't they simply refuse to be influenced?

NOVEMBER

7th

Off to Berlin after a good time in Shop-Window City. Mar was very good these last few days; they flew. I took the night train, started drinking again, smoked, scarcely slept, staggered out in the rain into the chilly morning with my two suitcases. The room hadn't yet been got ready: dark, cold, frightening. To Hedda's to collect my letters. Hedda seemed pretty sure of herself, alien, remote. Above all, a letter from Bi: she has been pregnant for at least two months. It was a good letter, full of composure and love, without a single murmur of complaint; reading it I loved her very much and was inordinately frightened. Wrote off to Otto and Cas the same day. Had been out of touch for a month, unable to reply to her. For the next few days I was on my own, it rained, the devil has taken up his winter quarters in me. On the third day I ate at Warschauer's. Then a letter arrived from Bi, it's all allright, she has been able to manage on her own. I breathed once more; reverently I read Otto's letter, which I shall always be grateful for, strong, simple, sure. He's seeing to everything ('no call to worry'). And there was I having annexed his hat and shoes, horror that I am. On the fifth day I met Hedda. In a good temper due to my letters. I kept laughing, she talked about responsibilities, wanted to kiss me, I discouraged it. She is stronger, has a success to her name, is loved. I met him at the place of some sculptor called Isenstein.[14] A strong young man with a thick head, rather a brutal face, slow, tough, bourgeois. I've nothing against him. He stood half behind her, half thrusting against her, his hand in his trouser pocket, snorting through his nostrils. I should think she *had* got responsibilities ...

12th

It's a grey city, a good city, I'm stumbling through it as best I can. Here's coldness, pitch in! Lunch at Warschauer's, bread and sausage for supper. Have been writing ballads. On my own. Asked He to come to the theatre, once she couldn't, the second time she sent a telephone message to say it was off. I find impoliteness much more wounding than deliberate malice, I shan't ring her again. For

[14] Isenstein. Not identified.

one thing I think her feelings have worn out from not being properly looked after, for another she has got embroiled in sordid computation, and for a third she is altogether second-rate. (The other day she told me 'I've been in love with Mast, XY and Gert Ilo' – I suppose I came next. And she always tagged along . . .). All the same she looks strong and healthy, better than when she was with me, that's the main thing.

Wednesday 16th

Visits. To Tschechowa, the Russian film actress,[15] and was struck by her expressiveness and truthfulness; I left my film there for her man.[16] It's perhaps to my disadvantage that being with good people always makes me childish, open and ready to confide, likewise cheeky. Secondly to H. **Kasack** at Potsdam, I spent an evening there too. He read some stuff by a certain Kulka,[17] bad artificial literary man's small talk; then followed up with Loerke,[18] who's a lot better, basically not bad, but humourless, quite outrageously self-effacing and infected with incense. They are nice people, helpful and insignificant, full of delicate distinctions, a bit thin. Oh, the War! In the Sezession[19] you can see pictures by these undernourished specialists in hunger: debilitated figures on the Cross, typical little foetus shapes, 'pure spirit', alcohol kept strictly for pickling. Cries for a child go up from all quarters. This kind of literature results from the blockade. Shortage of raw material all round. No enterprise. Verbal diarrhoea. And monologues, sexual stimulation, nothing but patients ... When does one's body get delivered up to sensation? When it's ill. They abandon themselves to emotion. And yet visions aren't at all the same thing as emotions or non-sense-impressions, nor is this cult of sterile idols comparable with the morphia of the word. The healer's art is a cynical one. Dying people are cynics, if they have it in them.

[15] Olga Tschechowa, ex-wife of Michael Chekhov, arrived from Russia in 1921 and has been a leading German film actress ever since.

[16] her man. Not hers but her flat-mate's: a dramaturg called Jarosy.

[17] Georg Kulka, 1897–1929. Austrian Expressionist poet, who in 1922 was working on the production side of Kiepenheuer Verlag.

[18] Oskar Loerke was chief reader to the publisher S. Fischer from 1917 till his death in 1941, when Kasack succeeded him.

[19] Sezession. Berlin artists' society presided over by Max Liebermann.

Literature today is becoming a business for littérateurs, and what littérateurs! Those compassionate dramatists (Hauptmann, Ibsen and co.) were the beginning of the end. All that ensues is flat, featureless plays. (In other words, there's no way round them.) There's only one opinion about the people and events on stage, and that's the playwright's own. The stalls are taught to 'understand everything'. No passion is left in the pit. People go to these brothels to get rid of their urges.

18th

Shaved, froze, had lunch.

Telephone. Small talk. Visit. Streets.

Bassermann as Kean,[20] Klöpfer as Götz.[21] Dorsch in music-hall.[22] Chaplin (*The Cure* – as convict). I did some work on *Jungle*. Schemes for the Grosse Schauspielhaus.[23] Ballads (with music: You smoke, you abuse yourself etc.).[24] An evening at Kasack's. Nice people: literature, paper, horn-rimmed glasses, ideals, Bau W. [?], H. E. Jacob, the higher class of schmuck as foreseen by Molière, a precious salon philosopher, a fathead. Warschauer excellent as always. La Märker[25] was there reading hands ('you have a very healthy hand'). Much confusion, chaos. Dominant: a C (child), it's as though I already had a domestic establishment, she actually did say 'child'. Then an escape, dominated at present by several Ms and an H. Turbulent relations with a woman in early youth. Chaos till 30, then 5 years of domesticity, repose, development, encounters with people of significance. After that, severe illness, which is overcome, then a woman of significance whom I likewise don't stick with. Nothing about my profession there. It's not dominant. The life line amazingly sure, cold, clear,

[20] Albert Bassermann, 1867–1952, eminent stage and screen actor, played Kean in Dumas' play adapted by Edschmid for the Deutsches Theater.
[21] Eugen Klöpfer, 1886–1950, stage and screen actor. Later acted in the Nazi film of *Jew Süss*. Götz is the hero of Goethe's early play *Götz von Berlichingen* (1773).
[22] Käthe Dorsch, 1889–1957. In 1922 became an actress for the Barnowsky theatres in Berlin.
[23] Grosses Schauspialhaus. Reinhardt's mass theatre in Berlin, a converted circus building.
[24] 'You smoke, you abuse yourself' etc. is the start of 'About exertion' in *Poems 1913–1956* p. 96.
[25] Possibly Edith Maerker (b. 1896) at that time a singer at Wiesbaden.

healthy. An escape a little while ago, but some event put me back on the rails again. ('You do not appear to take anything all that tragically; it is as though so far nothing had concerned you all that much ...'.)

24th

One thing is present in *Jungle*: the city. Which has recaptured its wildness, its darkness and its mysteries. Just as *Baal* is a song of the countryside, its swansong. We are on the scent of a mythology here.

25th

Kasack once more, giving a reading from Reimann.[26] Likewise Jarosy/Tschechowa,[27] who commission a film. Then the Scala where Matray and Sterna[28] are dancing; then both of them at Maenz's.[29] Afternoon feeding time at the zoo; human apes the great attraction. Jessner's *Othello* (with Kortner, Hofer, Steinrück)[30] brilliant, thin, humourless. He is a graphic artist. I've been told by Klabund to go to E. Reiss,[31] they'll read my manuscripts. Ate at Warschauer's.

---

[26] Presumably the humorist Hans Reimann, 1889–1969.

[27] Jarosy. See note on Tschechowa.

[28] Ernst Matray and Katta Sterna were a dancing pair.

[29] Maenz. Berlin bar, called after its landlady Anne Maenz.

[30] Leopold Jessner, 1878–1945, director of the Berlin State Theatre from 1919 to 1930. Of the players in his *Othello* Johanna Hofer was Fritz Kortner's wife – both became close friends of Brecht's – while Albert Steinrück had helped direct the Bavarian state theatres under the Munich Soviet.

[31] Erich Reiss Verlag, a Berlin publishing firm.

DECEMBER

2nd

Spent the morning hunched in this icy dark cellar vacillating
between a film for Tschechowa and a play for Durieux[32] (*Joan*).
Meanwhile time was trickling away, I occupied it by smoking. I
wrote to Die Wende;[33] they can have *Baal*. To Bi, I want to hear
from her; to Feuchtwanger, what's going on in Mu[nich]? Then I
wandered over to Warschauer's, where I usually eat, and bought Bi
a pearl necklace for 10 (ten) marks on the way. After lunch I went
to the Romanisches Café to see Klabund, he having written to me.
He had with him a young Hebrew who told me to be at E. Reiss's
tomorrow at 12 to discuss an overall contract. Pushed off with
Klabund and a cheerful grey-haired gent to a boozer where I was
given sweet brandy. Then to the Blüthner-Saal where Matray and
Sterna were dancing to music by Jaap Kool. The whole party then
drove back to Warschauer's for supper. It was disgusting,
though: they treated me as if I wasn't there (all that chatter stifling
me...); I smoked in the next room or in the lavatory and soon
slipped away: I'm still en route for the sun. Footed it to Maenz's.
There I met Granach who was nice, introduced me at once to
Goldberg of the Tribüne,[34] fixed up readings. Half frozen, half
feverish, I walked home with a full head, an empty heart, utterly
discontented, utterly discontented.

3rd.

I'd like now to write *Joan* and get my hands free for the *Asphalt
Jungle* trilogy. Three plays for the Grosses Schauspielhaus: 1.
Mankind in Pursuit of Money. 2. Cold Chicago. 3. The Forest.[35]

---

[32] Tilla Durieux, 1880–   . Leading actress for Reinhardt and Brahm before
1914, wife of Paul Cassirer the publisher, instrumental in financing Piscator's
theatre in 1927.

[33] Die Wende. Munich publishers founded in 1917 by Paul Baumann.

[34] Tribüne. Small Berlin theatre, had staged some important Expressionist
premières.

[35] *Asphalt Jungle*. Nothing remains of 1 and 3. There are a very few notes for
Cold Chicago, but the reference to Jensen's novel *The Wheel* suggests that this
overlapped with the *Jungle* plan.

Relevant material: 1. Wu Wei from *Wang-lun,* also *Richard III.* 2. *The Wheel.* 3. The *Malvi* material. Werner Krauss.[36]

7th.

When We Dead Awaken,[37] a melodrama about impotence, twenty years after the event, an old man's Expressionism, silly stuff – with Durieux, a really great actress.

8th.

Went to the cinema this evening and didn't see what was being shown; that's to say I saw a woman thrashing a pig. But I was wondering what's going to happen to the Warschauers' maid, who lives and works in a hole, is consumptive, has no home, no man, never says a word for days on end, moreover it's a dark flat. And I no longer see where the great difference lies; far be it from me to feel pity, all I mean is how poor we are, ape-like and easily abused, wretched, hungry, submissive.

9th.

It's always bursting out: the anarchy in the breast, the spasm. Revulsion and despair. It's the coldness you find in your heart. You may laugh and mock at it, but it is present in the laughter and it feeds the mockery.

11th.

Grossmann has written to Kahane,[38] I myself to Reinhardt. Now I can attend rehearsals of *The Dream Play.* They last from 10.30 to don't know when. I left at four. Klöpfer acts the lawyer and makes a tremendous thing of it. – Warschauer has arranged with A. Engel of Oswald Films[39] that I am to be given a boost. Kiepenheuer, with whom I had tea, is pushing me into Terra Films. Reiss and Kiepen-

---

[36] Werner Krauss, 1884–1959, outstanding Expressionist actor, later in *Jud Süss* and other Nazi films.

[37] *When We Dead Awaken.* By Ibsen, opened at the Lessing-Theater, 2 December 1921.

[38] Stefan Grossmann, editor of the magazine *Das Tagebuch,* wrote to Arthur Kahane (1872–1932), the dramaturg of the Reinhardt theatres.

[39] Oswald Films. Firm founded in 1916 by Richard Oswald, 1880–1963. A. Engel has not been identified.

heuer have given me draft contracts. – Feilchenfeldt[40] asked me to
Cassirer's. – A week ago Saturday Hedda travelled out to Kasack's
with me; on the way she indulged in some crude thick-skinned
gymnastics, with the result that I clammed up and she turned back
at Potsdam. I watched her walking away down the platform
dressed in brown, small, awkward, in a hurry, with too large a
head, then I lost sight of her. – One evening a whole lot of us were
in a studio. I rapidly got drunk, filled up with brandy, red wine,
liqueurs, floated up to the ceiling, couldn't recall a single song.
Klabund sang at the piano, soldiers' and whores' songs, danced,
worked hard to fend off the women, who were crazy about him,
including the one with the black fur trimmings. None of them
caused my mouth to water. Esther, the Rose of Sharon,[41] ritually
but with a light foot bore her Assyrian head through that smoke-
filled dive; a Malay girl danced with me like a whore, we collapsed
on the coal box, then she sang French Chansons in a deep smoker's
contralto situated around the level of the tip of her heart, music-hall
songs accompanied with the bottom; after which H. E. Jacob and I
did the dance of the two (cushioned) hunchbacks. At one point
Klabund was sitting there in silence listening to me like somebody
who has put his coat on, got no itinerary, no money, no use for
either, but just listens: here are the first crude barbaric songs of the
new age, an age forged in iron. There was a contributor to *Die
Aktion*, likewise to a fancy-coloured honeymoon magazine for
women, who thinly and deliberately spewed gall, enjoying a
systematic debauch with the word 'shitface'. Jacob, that plump-
cheeked rubber ball, that trombone-blowing church angel, that
squelchy plum jam tart, parodied my rolled Rs and kept telling me:
'They *will* say Becht, it should be Brrrecht, same way as it should be
guitarr and Jarcob'. He had swilled one of his moist eyes in a glass
of red wine; there was a red drop dangling from his nose. Around
four I was still there in that lurching playbox playing the guitar and
singing. Up came Grete the married lady from the days of the Kapp
Putsch[42] and sat down facing me, saying 'You're the only one who
can tell me. What is the Fourth Dimension?' – 'Ah, yes, that's the

---

[40] Feilchenfeldt. Not identified.

[41] Rose of Sharon. Possibly Esther Warschauer.

[42] Kapp Putsch. Unsuccessful right-wing coup of March 1920. The married
lady has not been identified.

vital question. But I can't do it just now, I've been drinking.' 'Ah, yes, you can't do it just now.'

12th.

Went to the final rehearsal of *The Dream Play* and at last put my finger on the basic flaws that had been tormenting me, only I was numbed by the slickness of the scenes. It isn't a dream. Ought to be crooked, twisted, gnarled, horrible, a nightmare with something delicious about it, a divinity's nightmare. And proves to be something for the right-minded, not a curve in it. I traipsed home exhausted. Ate and drank and went to bed at 7.30. But they woke me up at 10, and I felt such a pain in me, like a watery jellyfish between the ribs, that I got up. There's no air in this city, you can't live in this place. It had tied a knot in my throat, I got up, fled to a restaurant, fled from the restaurant, tramped around in the icy moonlit night, crawled back here, don't feel like writing, must get back to bed, can't sleep.

19th.

Back to those apocalyptic ghostly storms, brushing the roofs with their warm wetness, the influenza weather that poisons one; you lay your eggs in the stove and smoke yourself to death. First thing in the morning you get a heart spasm, then begin prancing around as if made of glass, find you can't work because your room is icy cold. Tonight Marianne will be here, a barbaric pleasure, then everything will improve and acquire a meaning. I'd like to put on my hard hat, only it's raining and blowing, and I'd like to drink schnaps (have indeed bought some), only it makes one's breath smell. I can't work, merely sing chorales and Wedekind. Now *there's* an improving writer for you. Him, plus a revolver, plus taste rather than conscience: it's better than getting confirmed. Small talk is good too, there's too much interval between the star-studded skies. What a feeling for romance one has to have! Stones on flat soil: that makes a home; no, it's no home. What a lot of unfamiliar people, how uncertain the intervals... The lamp's burning low. I've a bit of a headache on the left side. Who's that with the headache? My father was here, we sat facing one another over a table in a pub, two people who belonged together, a vague relationship but one that says a lot where our sort are concerned.

He took a kind of solicitous interest in me, gave me 1000 marks, talked about his business, never asked how I was getting along with Marianne, told me there'd be ham and duck for Xmas, they'll send me some. Very cheering. He was almost polite, said 'I shan't be able to come all that soon'. Me: 'I'll wait'. Him: 'Yes, do that'; nor did he make many demands: 'Don't bother to come with me, don't wait till the train leaves'. Remarkable.

Poem

Someone may turn up from Tiflis and kill me off.
Then a day goes pale (in the air)
Which had been blue as your coffee cup.
The trembling of a few blades of grass, which I noticed long ago
Comes finally to an end.
A dead man who admittedly has rotted
Has nobody left who knows what he looked like
All points of reference having gone.
My tobacco smoke which has meanwhile been climbing through
A myriad heavens
Loses its faith in God
And
Many are rogering women, smoking, drinking, chatting and
Everything is quite allright.[43]

Another Poem

Once thought I'd like to die between sheets of my own
Now
I no longer straighten the pictures on the wall.
I let the shutters rot, open my bedroom to the rain
Wipe my mouth on another man's napkin.
I had a room four months without ever knowing
That its window had a view to the back of the house
(Though that's something I love...)
All this occurs
Because I so favour the provisional and don't altogether
Believe in myself.

[43] Early version of 'Second letter to the Muscovites' in *Poems 1913–1956* p. 80. Later called 'Epistle'. The word 'allright' is in English.

Therefore I take any lodging, and if I shiver I say:
I'm still shivering.
And so engrained is this attitude
That it allows me none the less to change my linen
Out of courtesy to the ladies (and because
One surely won't
Need linen for ever).[44]

Yet another Poem

I am quite convinced that it will be a fine
Day tomorrow
That sunshine follows rain
That my neighbour loves his daughter
And my enemy is a bad man.
Also that I am better off than almost anyone else
I do no doubt.
Also I have never been heard to say
Things used to be better, or
The human race is degenerating
Or there are no women *one* man can satisfy.
In all this
I am broader-minded, more trusting and politer than the
    discontented –
For all this
Seems to me to prove very little.[45]

21st.
Marianne is here. It's raining. My *Pension* is warm, we can go there.
She's not looking all that well, but that doesn't stop her getting
more beautiful. She sang Mahler at the piano. I rushed off to film
rehearsals. Etc., etc.

23rd.
Signed up with Erich Reiss. Monthly payments of 750 marks. 1.
Ballads. 2. Stories. 3. Garga. Zarek took me off to Hesterberg's,

[44] 'Once I thought' in *Poems 1913–1956* p. 82. Translation by Frank Jellinek.
[45] 'First letter to the Half-breeds' in *Poems 1913–1956* p. 79. Translation by
Frank Jellinek.

where I signed for six days (500 marks). Singing soldiers' ballads at the 'Wilde Bühne'.[46]

24th.

Since then we've been living at the Warschauers'. Their hospitality is positively Asiatic. We have a little tree all to ourselves. I gave M. a Turkish cigarette holder, an old one, gunmetal,[47] an iron chain, a handwritten ballad. She gave me *The Idiot*, a tie, a haversack, socks. We had supper with Warschauer, who gave me Wedekind's *Lute Songs.*

25th.

Marianne keeps saying how in spite of all she liked Recht after she had left me, that he was tremendously in love. This may be because I'm not getting down to work. She's been going to bars with Hagemann (and others, a married couple), he tried to kiss her in the car, she's written him a fan letter about some production or other. She's had a letter addressed to 'Marianne', a New Year invitation, a party of four, i.e. two couples. She must answer if he is not to make other arrangements. And then (simultaneously) an official letter saying her engagement probably won't be renewed.

31st.

With Marianne and the Warschauers to the Grosses Schauspielhaus: *Orpheus*. Followed by supper, champagne, smoking, heating up lead.[48] With that the year has ended.

---

[46] 'Wilde Bühne'. Newly opened cabaret beneath the Theater des Westens, run by the actress Trude Hesterberg (1897–1967).

[47] gunmetal. Literally: Tula metal.

[48] heating up lead. A New Year tradition in Germany: divining the future from the shapes made by molten lead. *Orpheus in the Underworld* with Max Pallenberg was Reinhardt's last production at the Grosses Schauspielhaus before giving it up.

1922

JANUARY

7th.
We spent another week talking, loving, sitting around. Then off she went and I plunged back into cold Chicago. Paddling with my hands and feet. First of all dealing with publishers. Reiss offered 750 marks, Kiepenheuer 800. Both want stage rights too. I've already signed up with Reiss, but took the contract back in order to show it to Kasack. I had also to talk to Dreimasken.⁴⁹ It seemed a good idea to ask them for 1000 a month for one year. I also pushed Kiepenheuer up to 1000. On top of that I got Kiepenheuer to leave Dreimasken the stage rights for my next plays. Dreimasken wavered, offered 500. I hadn't brought *Garga* with me, as I didn't want to let them have it. But stuck out for the 1000. Finally they agreed after I had talked them into a stupor.

Last day of January
Have suddenly begun pissing blood. I tried to go on living it up, went to the 'Blauer Vogel'⁵⁰ with Klabund, Hedda, **Bronnen**; but thereafter started getting unmistakeable messages from my vital parts. Spent two days by myself lying in my chilly bed, then Hedda and Bronnen turned up. On Monday Frank [Warschauer] took me to the Charité⁵¹ where Hedda had fixed it all with Wollheim.⁵² Meantime I rang Marianne, who had handed in her notice at Wiesbaden and arrived right away. She has made her home in a hotel.

⁴⁹ Dreimasken. The Munich publishers associated with Feuchtwanger.
⁵⁰ 'Blauer Vogel'. Literally 'Blue Bird': name of an émigré Russian troupe under Juschni.
⁵¹ Charité. Principal hospital in central Berlin.
⁵² Dr Ernst Wollheim, Hedda Kuhn's fiancé, then on the hospital staff and later an eminent medical professor.

FEBRUARY

10th.

This makes my third week between these white walls. Not a breath of wind. Marianne began by coming daily; however the third day she found Bi's letters in my room, and this fairly shook her, till in the end a doctor decided that her lung had been affected, and now she's in bed at the Warschauers'. On her own. Bronnen drops in nearly every day and has brought along a comedy called *Spiel mit der Bewegung* [*Game with Movement*]. It is powerful and attractive, handles language radically but is not so strong on the poetic and philosophical sides. For my part, aside from a number of short prose pieces, I've roughed out a play *Manuel,* or *Manuel Wasserschleiche* [*Manuel Watersnake*],[53] a kind of declaration of independence. Otherwise I've been reading, smoking and chatting to myself, casting the occasional very cool glance at the shadowy little vulture overhead, the possibility of TB.

Not many remarks about art have so gripped me as Meier-Graefe's comment on Delacroix: 'This is a case of a hot heart beating in a cold person'.

Any human being has to use his superior brain to deliver himself from forced labour. No kind of meanness is meaner than work. Nothing is more unworthy of a man than doing something from which he gets no enjoyment. The man of work is the slave who gets the credit, and the fact that humanity has always been bullied by slaves is irrelevant.

If one only had the courage it would be easy as pie to ascribe nearly every ideal and institution, not excluding a large proportion of those that have dug themselves in on Tahiti, to the human race's desperate need to conceal its true situation. Respect for the family, glorification of work, the lure of fame, likewise religion, philosophy, art, smoking, intoxication, aren't just isolated, clearly calculated and generally recognised *means* (moyens) of combating mankind's sense of isolation, abandonment and moral outlawry; but visible guarantees of an immense stockpile of values and securities. It is from this seductive cosiness that man's enslavement springs.

[53] *Manuel.* Only a short outline survives.

There is one common artistic error which I hope I've avoided in *Baal* and *Jungle*, that of trying to carry people away. Instinctively I've kept my distance and ensured that the stage realisation of my (poetical and philosophical) effects remains within bounds. The spectator's 'splendid isolation' is left intact, it is not *sua res quae agitur*, he is not fobbed off with an invitation to feel sympathetically, to fuse with the hero and cut a meaningful and indestructible figure while watching himself in two simultaneous versions. There is a higher type of interest to be got from making comparisons, from whatever is different, amazing, impossible to take in as a whole.

11th.

It's common for writers of tragedies to take sides with their hero, particularly towards the end. This is rubbish. They should be siding with Nature. In fact they are so scared of discrediting their hero that they daren't even ridicule Nature or convey that repulsive mooing you get from some idiot cow which has swallowed a grasshopper. Such is the bourgeoisie of the theatre!

Night. I've had a lungful of afternoon air: been to see Marianne, who's on her back at Warschauer's. She's heated and mistrustful. Tonight, Flaubert's letters.

12th.

These front-line despatches from a lunatic mammoth are mind-boggling. Who does he think he is? What a sinful, pig-headed, obsessional Gaul! What dedication to a job that must be handled with a light touch! How sure of his material this troglodyte must have been to risk investing so much effort in it! All we've been doing is frivolous stuff, monkey tricks, just by the way . . .

13th.

The drama is undoubtedly one symptom of a people's adolescence. As shown by Orge, whose philosophy is infinitely stronger and more mature than mine; it's of the idyllic variety. There's some compensation in the fact that plays like Shlink[54] bear, branded on their backs, the sign of the *last* of all the heroic idiocies. At the

[54] Shlink. I.e. *In the Jungle of Cities.*

moment the arena has been cleared for the powerful new plays of
the last set of idiots but one. If any of us succeeds in turning the
drama into a game without weakening it – something perhaps that
calls not so much for a heroic religion, as in the case of the great
Greek tragedies, as for a powerful and consistent philosophy –
then we shall evade the general laughter with a grimace.

14th.
Bronnen's comedy: strong on construction but weak in ideas and
thin on the cosmic side, more epic than dramatic, though each
scene stands up and the whole thing gives much pleasure.

16th.
It's surely like this: there *is* no 'other side'. And those people
whose love is based on hoping for one, amid poverty and
deprivation, have their hope, for the 'other side' doesn't exist. But
those who are aware of this and want to have their paradise on this
side will find out that isn't one.

In the Jungle
Bronnen
Charité
Jessner
Cold Chicago
Jottings.

ABOUT 1921, UNDATED.

Shortly before dawn I had a dream that disturbed me for hours by
its exceptional realism and unexpectedness. We were among a fair-
sized party of people, and wishing at length to be alone I cunningly
pushed Otto and various others into an overcrowded automobile.
After a while they drove off and M. and I went back inside. Hardly
had we arrived upstairs than I heard rapid weighty steps on the
stairway, which much annoyed me since I at once assumed that
Otto was yet again unable to stand being on his own; so I was not
surprised to find that it was indeed Otto. He however walked
swiftly past me with a red face, not looking at me, up to the
corridor window, which gave on to a deep dark light-well; peered
hurriedly into this, bent forward, stepped without a word on to the
windowsill, passing me in one single giant stride from the stairway
across the corridor, and, with an expression of as much
thoughtfulness as his haste allowed, leapt down it. I was terribly
scared, hugged Marianne and thought 'So it has come to this?'.

The principal characters

Aman. See Rosmarie.

Banholzer. See Bi, Frank.

Bi. Paula Banholzer, also nicknamed Bittersweet. One of three daughters of an Augsburg doctor. Introduced to Brecht by Otto Müllereisert about 1915. Bore his illegitimate son Frank at her parents' house in the Algäu in July 1919. Took a job in an Augsburg bank. Married Hermann Gross in March 1924. Is still living in Augsburg, where she and Brecht again met after the Second World War.

Brecht, Berthold, Sophie (Brezing), and Walter. See Father, Mama, Walter.

Bronnen. Arnolt Bronnen, 1895–1959, Austrian playwright. Wounded and taken prisoner on the Italian front; thereafter to Berlin where he worked for Wertheim's stores. Met Brecht at the home of Otto Zarek's parents in December 1921; allowed him to direct *Vatermord* (Bronnen's first play) till the actors rebelled. Collaborated with him on *Robinsonade auf Asuncion*, story submitted to Oswald-Film for a 100,000 mark prize. Worked in films for Joe May and Erich Pommer; became a nationalist, then a Nazi, and returned to Berlin after the Second World War as a communist supporter after briefly directing the Scala Theatre in Vienna. His memoir *Tage mit Bertolt Brecht* appeared in 1960.

Brüstle. Dr Wilhelm Brüstle, editor of the weekly literary supplement (*Der Erzähler*) to the *Augsburger Neueste Nachrichten*, which printed some of the schoolboy Brecht's poems between 1914–16, also his obituary for Wedekind in March 1918.

Buschiri. See Otto Müllereisert.

Cas. Rudolf Caspar Neher, 11 April 1897–30 June 1962. Son of a teacher at the Roten-Tor-Schule, Augsburg; brother of Marietta Neher (Ortner); no relative of the actress Carola Neher. School friend and classmate of Brecht's from 1911–14, then to the Munich Kunstgewerbeschule, developed into the finest stage designer of his generation. Called up into the army on 21 June 1915; served on the Western front, where he was once buried alive. Saw much of Brecht again from early 1919 on, being closely involved in the discussion and revision of *Baal* and *Drums in the Night*, also designing the Munich production of *In the Jungle* in 1923. Established himself in Berlin c. 1922–23, worked for the Deutsches Theater and Staatstheater and on all important Brecht productions till 1933. Remained in Germany under the Nazis but renewed the association with Brecht after the latter's return in 1947, notably as co-director of *Antigone* (1948) and Lenz's *The Tutor* (1950).

Fanny. Franziska ('Fannerl') Pfanzelt, subsequently wife of 'Orge'. Worked from 1917–23 with Käthe Hupfauer and Ida Grassold in Steinicke's lending library on the Ludwigstrasse, Augsburg, an establishment much frequented by Brecht and his friends. The owner, Alfred Kathan, also ran a section of erotica at another address.

Father, Papa. Berthold Friedrich Brecht, son of a lithographic printer, born in Achern (about half way between Baden-Baden and Strasbourg) on 6 November 1869. Worked for a firm of paper merchants in Stuttgart, then moved to Augsburg in 1893 as employee of the Haindl paper mills which had been founded there in 1849. Married Sophie Brezing on 15 May 1897. They lived first in a flat at 7, Auf dem Rain, then moved to a company-owned house at 2, Bleichstrasse. He became a director of the firm in 1914. Remained in Augsburg after his son's emigration in 1933, when he helped him to buy his house in Denmark. Died on 20 May 1939.

Feuchtwanger. Dr Lion Feuchtwanger, 1884–1958, Author of *Jew Süss*, one of the best-known German writers of his day. Living in Munich when Brecht approached him in March 1919 for help in placing *Drums in the Night*. Then a dramaturg at the Kammerspiele and a reader for the Dreimasken publishing firm, he made Brecht his protégé and became a lifelong friend. The two men collaborated in 1923–24 on the adaptation of Marlowe's *Edward II* and thereafter on the revision of Feuchtwanger's play *Kalkutta 4 Mai* (1925), the editing of the Moscow-based émigré magazine *Das Wort* (1936–39) and the writing of *The Visions of Simone Machard* (1942–43) in California, where they were neighbours from 1941 until Brecht's return to Europe.

Mrs Feuchtwanger. Dr Martha Feuchtwanger, wife of the above. Drew Brecht's attention to the reports of the case of Josef Apfelböck in August 1919 and received the dedication of his ensuing ballad. On the Kammerspiele objecting to the too 'political' title of Brecht's *Spartakus* drama she suggested changing it to *Drums in the Night*. A good skier and climber, she helped her husband escape from French internment in the Second World War, and now lives in their California home.

Frank. Frank Walter Otto Banholzer, son of Brecht and Paula Banholzer. Born at Kimratshofen 30 July 1919 and christened after Frank Wedekind, Walter Brecht and Otto Müllereisert who, with Caspar Neher, was his godfather. Brought up for the first three years by a local roadmender's family and thereafter by peasants, he was taken to Augsburg by his mother and then, after her marriage, looked after near Vienna by relatives of Helene Weigel, Brecht's second wife. He returned to Augsburg in 1935 and was called up in the·German army during the Second World War. In November 1943 he was killed in an air raid on the Russian front.

Frank (p. 157). See Warschauer.

George. See Orge.

Granach. Alexander Granach, 1880–1949, born at Werbowitz in Galicia, a leading German actor at Reinhardt's and other Berlin theatres before 1933. Was Kragler in the Berlin production of *Drums in the Night*, also playing in *Die Massnahme* (1930) and Brecht's own Berlin production of *Mann ist Mann* (1931). Played the lead in Toller's *Hoppla, wir leben!* with Piscator's first company in 1927, and was in *Nosferatu, Kameradschaft* and many other films. His memoirs *There Goes an Actor* appeared in New York in 1943.

Hartmann. Rudolf Hartmann, born Augsburg 18 May 1898, son of a postal official. School contemporary and classmate of Brecht's, cousin of Ernestine Müller who was recipient of some of Brecht's early poems (since lost). Played the guitar and took part in Brecht's serenading expeditions and visits to the fairground. Later read Law and became official prosecutor in the local courts.

He, Hedda. Hedda Kuhn from Rastatt near Baden-Baden. Medical student at Munich university, where she met Brecht in the autumn of 1917 after one of Kutscher's seminars (see note p. 83); also knew Warschauer and Zarek. Left Munich at the time of the Soviet republic in spring 1919 and studied for a term at Freiburg. Moved to Berlin, where Brecht saw her in February 1920. Helped in his first negotiations with Kasack (q.v.) at Kiepenheuer-Verlag and introduced him to the students' club where he met Klabund. The end of their affair is commemorated by the 'Psalm' 'Of He' (*Poems 1913–1956*, p. 41). The following winter it was her fiancé Dr Ernst Wollheim who treated Brecht during his illness in Berlin, taking him into the Charité hospital where he was working (on condition that she should *not* visit the invalid). They married in March 1922. Professor Wollheim, now an internationally eminent cardiologist, has taught at Würzburg university since 1948 and was its Rector in 1963–64.

Hei, Heigei. See Otto Müllereisert.

Jacob. Heinrich Eduard Jacob, 1889–1967. Novelist and story writer. An early contributor to the Expressionist journals *Der Sturm* and *Die Aktion*. As editor of the Berlin literary magazine *Der Feuerreiter* (1921–23) he published Brecht's story 'Ein gemeiner Kerl' – which seems to have been derived from a lost one-act play called *Der Schweinigel* – in April 1922 and his poem 'Of Cortez's Men' in December of the same year. The latter was also included in Jacob's anthology *Verse der Lebenden* which appeared from Propyläen-Verlag a few years later. He became Vienna correspondent of the *Berliner Tageblatt*, then emigrated to the US.

Kasack, Hermann, 24 July 1896–10 January 1966. In 1920 became a publisher's reader for Gustav Kiepenheuer's firm in Potsdam, who in 1922 published Brecht's *Baal* and were expecting to follow with *Die Hauspostille* (*Devotions for the Home*), his first book of verse. By 1925, when Brecht took this book away from them, Kasack had left, thereafter working for S. Fischer (briefly) and as a freelance writer. In 1933 the Nazis forbade him to publish, but in 1941 Peter Suhrkamp (see note on p. 9) took him on as chief reader for S. Fischer's former firm, where he remained till 1949, the year when they published *Mother Courage*. He is best known for his own novel *Die Stadt hinter dem Strom*, which appeared in 1947.

Klabund, real name Alfred Henschke, son of a chemist, born near

Frankfurt on the Oder on 4 November 1890. Started publishing poems in 1913 and soon became known as a prolific ballad writer and singer in the tradition of Frank Wedekind. Took part in *Die Rote Zibebe*, the late-night entertainment following the first two performances of *Drums in the Night*. In 1924 his adaptation of the Chinese story *The Chalk Circle* was a great success at the Deutsches Theater; this was the start of Brecht's interest in the same theme. He married the Munich actress Carola Neher (unrelated to Caspar Neher) who later played Polly in Pabst's *Threepenny Opera* film. He died of TB in Davos on 14 August 1928.

Kuhn. See He, Hedda.

Lud. Ludwig Prestel, born in 1900, one of two sons of an Augsburg stock-keeper. Met Brecht through his elder brother Rudolf, a friend and classmate of the poet. Was a good pianist, sometimes playing duets with Pfanzelt. Often accompanied Brecht on the guitar; said to have written tunes for 'The legend of the harlot Evelyn Roe' (1917) and 'The ballad of Hannah Cash' (1921) (both in *Poems 1913–1956*). Also collaborated on Baal's song 'If a woman's hips are ample' in the 1918 version of the play.

Ma, Mar. Marianne Zoff, Brecht's first wife and mother of his elder daughter Hanne. Was a Viennese opera singer engaged by the Augsburg municipal theatre from September 1919 to sing various rôles. After her last appearance there in mid-May 1921 she moved to Bad Reichenhall, then to the Wiesbaden opera for the 1921–22 season, but broke her contract there when Brecht fell ill in Berlin. The couple were married in Munich on 3 November 1922, when she was already expecting their daughter, born the following March. They set up house in Munich in a flat in the Akademiestrasse, but by 1924 the marriage was already breaking up. That autumn he moved to Berlin and she resumed her career, singing at various West German theatres. On 2 November 1927 their marriage was dissolved and during 1928 she married the actor Theo Lingen.

Mama. Wilhelmine Friederike Sophie Brecht, born Sophie Brezing. Brecht's mother, born near Bad Waldsee some 50 miles south of Ulm on 8 September 1871, daughter of a stationmaster. A protestant, she married her catholic husband in 1897 in a protestant ceremony and had her elder son baptised protestant. Began showing symptoms of breast cancer around 1910, was seriously ill by 1917 and died on 1 May 1920, six weeks before the first entry in the Diaries.

Marie, Fräulein Marie. Maria Roecker, housekeeper to Brecht's parents from 1910–39. Various accounts suggest that she was not well disposed towards Brecht.

Müllereisert. See Otto.

Orge. Georg Pfanzelt, four and a half years older than Brecht and one of his closest Augsburg friends, a good pianist whom he respected for his critical judgement and musical gifts. Exempted from war service because of a club foot. Studied local government and became a hospital administrator in Augsburg. Lover of Fanny, q.v. Brecht alluded to him in a number of the early songs and poems, notably 'Orge's List of wishes', 'Orge's reply on being sent a soaped noose' (both in *Poems 1913–1956*) and 'Orge's Song' in scene 3 of *Baal*, whose first edition (1922) was dedicated to him.

Otto. Otto Müller, known as Müllereisert. Also nicknamed 'Hei', 'Heigei' and 'Buschiri'. Two and a half years younger than Brecht, and among his closest lifelong friends. Attended St Stephans-Gymnasium till end of 1917 when he joined the 4th Artillery Regiment as an officer cadet. In April 1919 he joined the 'Volkswehr' to combat the Munich Soviet, fought under General von Epp and was lightly wounded. Was godfather to Frank Banholzer and a witness at Brecht's marriage to Marianne Zoff. Later practised as a doctor in Berlin, where he helped get Brecht's furniture out to Denmark in 1933 and signed his death certificate in 1956.

Papa. See Father.

Pfanzelt. See Fanny, Orge.

Prestel. See Lud.

Recht. Marianne Zoff's lover before Brecht. Subject of the latter's satire 'Vom verliebten Schwein Malchus' (German and English texts in *Manual of Piety*). Is said to have been a manufacturer of playing-cards from Bad Reichenhall near Salzburg.

Roecker. See Marie.

Rosmarie, Rosie. Marie Rose (or Rose Marie) Aman, Augsburg hairdresser's daughter, who met Brecht in 1916 when at the Englisches Institut girls' school. Claimed that Brecht gave her her first kiss. Is supposed to have been the subject of his song 'Remembering Marie A.' (*Poems 1913–1956*, p. 35). Later became Mrs Eigen, and was still living in Augsburg in the 1960s.

Walter. Brecht's younger brother, born in Augsburg on 29 June 1900. Attended the Barfüsserschule in that city, followed by the Oberrealschule in the Katharinengasse. Called up in the 3rd Infantry Regiment in autumn 1917. Joined the Volkswehr in spring 1919 and took part in the suppression of the Munich Soviet. Played the piano and is said to have devised the tunes for some of Brecht's early poems. After 1919 he studied paper technology at the Darmstadt Technische Hochschule and in the United States; then joined his father at the Haindl paper mills, becoming managing director in August 1926. In 1931 he became the first professor of paper technology at the Darmstadt TH, where he remained till 1971, serving as Rector in 1956–57.

Warschauer. Frank Warschauer, born in Darmstadt 22 April 1892, a nephew of the historical writer Emil Ludwig. Poet and film critic, a sub-editor on the music magazine *Anbruch* and contributor to *Die Weltbühne*. Studies in Munich, where he met Brecht through Hedda Kuhn. Brecht stayed with him during his Berlin visit of February–March 1920. Reported to have killed himself in Holland 18 May 1940 at the time of the Nazi invasion. Brecht later described him as 'highly sensitive and not very productive' (diary note of 24 January 1942).

Zarek, Otto. Born 20 February 1898, ten days after Brecht. Son of a Berlin business man. Read law at Munich university and attended Arthur Kutscher's seminar (see footnote to p. 83). Introduced to Brecht by Hedda Kuhn in the winter of 1918–19. Dramaturg at the Munich Kammerspiele from 1921–25, then to Berlin as chief dramaturg to the theatre director Felix Saltenburg. His play *David* was published in 1921. Emigrated in 1933 and returned to Germany in 1954, dying there on 21 August 1958.

Zoff, Otto. Born Prague 9 April 1890. Marianne's brother. Austrian playwright and novelist. Was a publisher's reader for S. Fischer and a dramaturg in Munich and Breslau during the 1920s. In 1932 moved to Hungary, then Italy; emigrated to the US in 1941. After the Second World War he returned to Germany, where he died in Munich in 1963.

Index